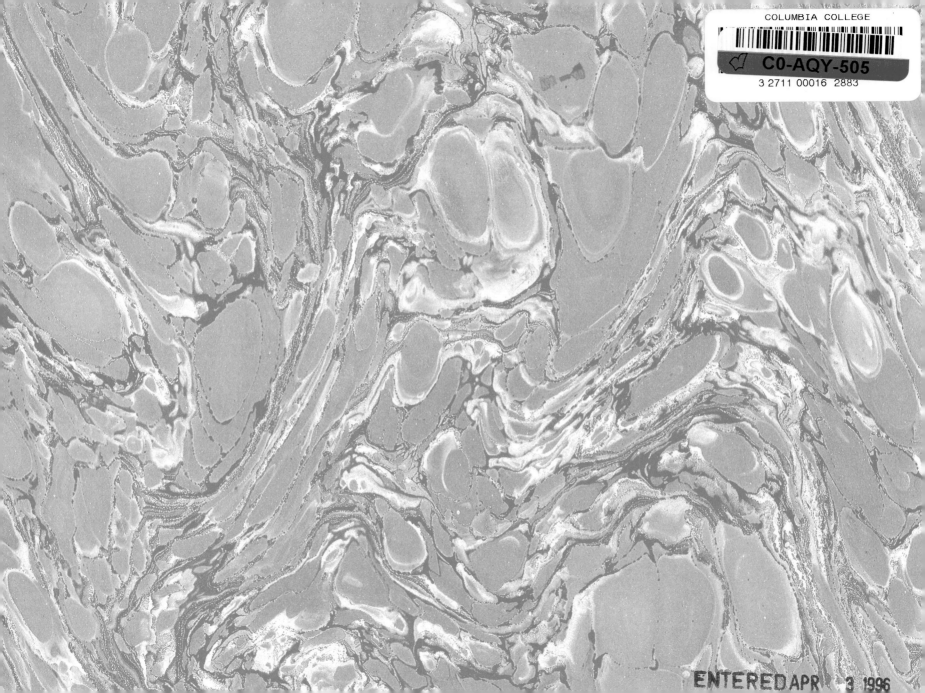

APR 0 6 2000			

DEMCO 38-297

THE
VICTORIAN CATALOGUE
OF
HOUSEHOLD FURNISHINGS

Hampton & Sons' Pall Mall East Premises.

THE
VICTORIAN CATALOGUE
OF
HOUSEHOLD FURNISHINGS

INTRODUCTION BY
STEPHEN CALLOWAY

STUDIO
EDITIONS

The Victorian Catalogue of
Household Furnishings

This edition published in 1994 by Studio Editions
Ltd, Princess House, 50 Eastcastle Street, London
W1N 7AP, England

ISBN 1 85891 125 7
Printed in Singapore

INTRODUCTION

STEPHEN CALLOWAY

It is exactly a century ago that Hamptons, one of the largest and most celebrated of household furnishing, stores in London, issued a substantial and lavishly illustrated catalogue proudly offering their wares. Even in an era of expensively produced trade catalogues, its publication was of considerable interest at the time, and the *Illustrated London News*, the foremost pictorial journal of the day, carried the following appreciation of Hampton's volume on September 1st 1894, in a short notice of the firm's contribution to a small international exhibition of furnishings:

> 'Not the least remarkable item of Hampton and Son's exhibit (at Antwerp) is their recently issued "Book of Specimen Interiors and Furniture". A glance through this volume reveals at once the real source of Messrs. Hampton and Son's success as furnishers, as the contents show that rooms can nowadays be furnished in a quite elegant manner at a comparatively trifling outlay. It is by their skill in achieving this end that Hampton and Sons have built up their immense business, and that this book of examples affords ample evidence of the fact that it is upon this ability to put a tastefully furnished Home within the reach of the most modest income that the House still relies for its chief support.'

The firm of Hamptons was established in 1830, the year in which George IV died, and at a period when great changes both in artistic taste and in the organisation and workings of the furniture trade were beginning to alter the whole pattern of home furnishings. With the gradual decline in the importance of the old order of the aristocracy with its traditions of grand patronage, and with the increasingly rapid rise of a new, energetic and aspirational middle class, a new market force ambitious to display a new and hard-won status in material terms, retailers came to occupy an ever more crucial position in the supply of domestic furniture. All over England, in the major provincial cities and larger towns, but more especially in London, emporia offering furniture and other items of a more or less fashionable and artistic nature were beginning to be an important feature of the urban scene.

By the middle years of the nineteenth century, the successful mercantile classes had made 'shopping', as we understand the term – that is the choosing and buying of ready-made items – as important, even in the fashionable world, as the old system of bespeaking furniture and other goods for the decoration of houses. This was the period which saw the great rise, in London, in Paris and throughout civilized Europe, of entirely new ways of life and the first glimmerings of what we can begin to recognize as the origins of our own form of 'consumer society.' New patterns of trade and, in particular, novel types of retail premises arose to cater to a developing bourgeois clientele which preferred the comfortable certainty of inspecting a retailer's stock of items which could be purchased instantly, rather than ordering things to be made and awaiting their delivery.

Throughout the 1830s and 40s and on into the succeeding decades, shopping arcades became the popular haunts of the well-to-do and the idle lounger in search of amusement and the smaller sort of luxury goods. More substantial things were to be found in the new department stores, such as Samaritaine, which appeared first around the middle years of the century in France, and which rapidly grew to become shopping establishments on an entirely unprecedented scale in terms of their architecture, their range of merchandise and their vast turnover. Gradually, too, more specialized firms, such as those originally dealing exclusively in home furnishings, tended to follow the trend of these first great department stores and become more comprehensive in their approach to supplying the needs of their customers. Many, including Hamptons, extended their stock to include not just furniture and decorative objects, but also small carpets and rugs, curtains and all manner of smaller goods from lamps, tablewares and kitchen items, through to bathroom fittings and domestic gadgets on the one hand, and exotic collector's pieces on the other.

By the latter decades of the century, and with an enormous increase in the volume of trade, the pattern of big stores selling furniture was well established in London. Most of the main firms operated upon broadly similar lines, controlling the overall look of the pieces they offered, but more often than not dividing the actual manufacture of their various wares between their own workshops and those of the smaller traditional cabinet-making firms, which at that date remained plentiful in several areas of the city. The concentration of such little, individual firms and workshops around the Tottenham Court Road area may in part explain why a number of the larger old stores were gathered there. In the heyday of the trade, at the turn of the century, Maples, James Schoolbred, Oetzmann (formerly of Hampstead Road) and, more latterly, Ambrose Heal were all to be found within a few hundred yards of each other in this previously unprepossessing area. A second well-known enclave of specialist cabinet-makers and general furniture workshops once existed in Soho, especially in and around Wardour Street, which had a reputation for the supply of a certain sort of rather theatrical, and usually bogus antique furniture. Much of the self-consciously artistic furniture sold by Arthur Lazenby Liberty at his famous Regent Street shop, established in 1875, was also made by small independent craftsman in this area, working to designs from the Liberty design studio.

Although Hamptons' large and rambling premises lay to the south of this general area and at not great distance from the great shopping streets of the day, their position must have always given the store something of the feeling of being an outlier from the main paths of London's growing army of shoppers. Situated close to the more traditionally aristocratic haunts of the Metropolis in Pall Mall and the Haymarket, and nearer to the centre of the fashionable West End of the late eighteenth century or of the days of Beau Brummell, the firm's address of course reflects quite clearly the date of its founding in 1830. Nevertheless, in spite of the shift which had tended to draw retail business away to the West and North, leaving Hamptons as almost the only shop, let alone large store, in the immediate vicinity, the firm had continued to prosper.

Indeed by 1894, the year in which the present catalogue was issued, photographs and illustrations reveal that the firm had consolidated its position to such an extent that the store had grown to occupy an entire block fronting onto Pall Mall East. In fact, the company's rather heterogeneous property embraced a number of different original buildings, some of which Hamptons held on Crown leases, but others of which were freeholds; an anomalous situation which continued to affect the fate of the site for many years, but which had not prevented the firm from creating, probably by about 1855-60, a more or less unified street frontage of shop windows running along two sides, and interrupted only by the tall fluted columns of the earlier projecting entrance porch which survived at the Eastern end of the front, the earliest part of the group of buildings.

Above each of the full-length, plate-glass shop windows, both on the main Pall Mall East front and stretching some way down the side-street facade, ran a fascia with the name Hampton & Sons Cabinet Makers repeated in handsome lettering in gold-against black *verre eglomisé*, whilst in the typical style of the grander mid- and later nineteenth-century shop-fronts of London and Paris, heavy gilded brass letters on the low, sloping sills of the windows spelled out the firm's other specialities such as Carpet Manufacturers. The facades of the upper floors, though varying in date between the 1830s and 1860s were finished in a unifying pale stucco, their regular fenestration broken only at the Western corner, nearest to the Pall Mall side, by two unusually large display windows. In the photograph reproduced in the catalogue which shows the store as it appeared in the 1890s, the shop windows can be clearly seen; they are dressed in the manner of the day with a considerable profusion of items, somewhat heaped together rather than more elegantly spaced out, but all backed with swathes of the same furnishing fabric, which again has the effect of unifying the appearance of the long front and side elevations of the store.

As the *Illustrated London News* article had suggested, not the least appeal of the Hampton's store lay in its remarkable comprehensiveness, allied to a subtly implied reassurance that the goods offered combined a degree of tastefulness with affordable value. These factors were especially crucial in this period, for besides the perennial concerns of the careful customer for quality and price, the ordinary householder of the late nineteenth century was obsessed with a set of often ill-digested notions of what constituted the 'artistic interior'. Faced with the great multiplicity of possible styles, the average customer craved guidance and, if possible, some guarantee of 'good taste'.

The title-page of the 1894 catalogue proclaimed that it was 'Illustrated with fifty collotype Reproductions of Artistic Interiors, in various styles, specially designed for this work'; whilst these were accompanied in the main body of the publication by 'upwards of 2,000 Half-tone blocks of Furniture Photographed from Stock, and many Coloured Illustrations of Carpets, Curtains, Linens, Blinds, China and Glass', it is the views of complete schemes which obviously tell us most about the decorative ideals of the day. However, with the precise information about the styles, material and prices of individual pieces itemized throughout the rest of the catalogue we can build up a far more minutely detailed picture of the rooms of the period than could ever be derived from the study of illustrations of complete interiors alone. It is because of the vast and almost unparalleled scope of the Hampton's catalogue that it opens such a fascinating and illuminating window into the world of the late nineteenth-century interior; these remarkable illustrations show in page after page the minutiae of the Victorian home, allowing us to form a highly focussed picture of the domestic aspirations and often rather muddled artistic notions which governed the choice and arrangement of the better sort of ordinary houses throughout the period.

The main style statements revealed by the catalogue are of course to be found in the group of illustrations of complete rooms in which items from the store's stock are shown in suggested arrangements and in conjunction with schemes of decoration appropriate to each look. Printed by the newly available collotype process which was particularly suited to the reproduction of the subtle tones of a wash-drawing, these highly detailed images cannot unfortunately be ascribed to any particular artist, since they are signed not with the painter's names, but merely Hampton and Sons, a convention of the day observed in most trade catalogues and also, generally, in the proposal drawings prepared by all kinds of commercial firms and submitted to their clients. What is revealed immediately is the extent of the great divide that existed at this date between the taste and styles considered appropriate for what we might term 'polite' furniture and furnishings - that is to say, pieces for display and the creation of comfort and effect in the drawing-room and other more important rooms of the house, nearly all of which is in a variety of period styles - and the contrastingly simpler, more practical sorts of things intended for the service areas of the home. These tend, by comparison, to aim at modernity and efficiency and eschew the more obvious and flamboyant decoration of those items made more clearly to impress. What is, perhaps, quite surprising is the extent to which in both these categories, but most obviously in the area of polite furniture, the ordinary bourgeois home failed to reflect to any serious degree the true aesthetic influence of the radical artistic movements that had changed the face of design at the top end of the market. What we see here is the comfortable middle-ground of furnishing; things of good intrinsic quality made to please a clientele living in ordinary houses and seeking a degree of modest, yet always discreet grandeur that would prove consistent with comfort and lasting use.

Stylistically, as might be expected at this date and in this milieu, these interiors are almost all historicising to some degree. Significantly, only the cheapest are in a 'modern' style that does not aim to strike an exact period note. All those with any greater pretentions to style and grandeur are based on the past. In this they offer us precise clues about the taste of the day, for they range freely through all the various periods that were most admired at the time from Elizabethan or Flemish Renaissance, through the various English styles of the seventeenth and eighteenth centuries, including a barbarous 'Queen Anne' manner and a sort of Chippendale Chinoiserie, and on up to what was ubiquitously known as 'Adams Style'. These English decorative conventions are also interspersed with curious versions of the French Louis XV and Louis XVI manners as they were understood, or rather misunderstood at the time. Some of these specific styles might be quite difficult to identify without their captions, so generalized are many of the elements. What they all share, however, are a highly consistent density and a heaviness of ornament that instantly proclaim their true date, whether they in fact aim at the whimsicality of the French or English Rococo or the solidity of the earlier eras.

Beyond what we may discover in general about the preferred styles of the past as applied to the decoration of the late nineteenth-century English house, another rather more precise aspect of this historicising taste may also be deduced from a careful perusal of the catalogue; and that is the relatively rigid notions at the time concerning which of the styles of the past were appropriate to the various different parts of the house. Thus it becomes clear that the Elizabethan or contemporary Flemish styles were considered to be rugged and handsome in a way that made them suitable for the hall or other semi-public parts such as the dining-room. Queen Anne and Georgian were perceived as sound, 'good taste' styles that befitted the drawing room, even though a slightly more frivolous Rococo or Chinoiserie note could also be struck with propriety in a room in which pleasant company might seek a degree of softness and comfort. Of the French styles, Louis XVI was again thought of as a drawing room manner, whilst the more feminine and curvaceous Louise XV was perhaps more fittingly employed in rooms such as the private sitting-room or boudoir which were often considered the domain of the woman of the house and used for the reception of only her more intimate friends.

In the preface to the catalogue we read that 'The designs selected for illustration may, without exception, be regarded as representing the current taste in the matter of style'. In fact, in general both the individual roomsets and the pages of specific pieces in the catalogue reveal a somewhat conservative taste for their day. The actual items offered are, in many cases, even a little old-fashioned, reflecting to quite an extent the preferences first made popular by the protaganists of the Aesthetic Movement of the 1870s and 1880s. One page of chairs, for example, is quite clearly influenced by the elegant, turned stick 'Sussex' chairs popularised and sold for twenty years by William Morris through his 'art-furnishing' business, Morris & Co. However, what is also interesting is what is not shown. There is for example almost nothing that reflects the taste for extremely simplified Japanese forms in furniture as designed by Godwin and others and manufactured in ebony by the 'Art-furniture' maker William Watt, and neither, it seems, was there any room among the highly finished surfaces of this commercial sort of furniture for anything that reflected the deliberately rougher, more natural styling and finish of the romantic, Pre-Raphaelite-inspired products of the Arts and Crafts Movement. Even more tellingly, there is practically no hint of the more recent developments of English and Continental designers working in the Art Nouveau style. This is not entirely surprising, for this kind of avant-garde work was often held to be both too shocking and too decadent for the English home. Indeed, when a group of pieces in this novel style was offered to the Victoria and Albert Museum at the turn of the century, the museum authorities thought it prudent almost to hide this dangerously radical little collection away from the main galleries, out at the museum's Bethnal Green outstation, lest right-minded makers should have their tastes corrupted by the extravagant forms and wickedly sinuous lines of these bizarre, and all too 'foreign' tables and chairs.

It was, as the preface to the catalogue pointed out, precisely because of the very popular or, as it might be said, very safe nature of the goods offered, that turnover was so high; as a result, therefore, the firm was enabled to buy materials in considerable bulk and thus minimise costs for high quality articles. Also, somewhat against the prevailing pretence of the day, the catalogue proudly proclaimed that all the furniture that was made in Hampton's own workshops (removed by this date to Belvedere Road in South East London) was created with use of 'all the latest machinery for preparing the woods and other material'; it was thought expedient however, to add that every piece was nonetheless 'finished by hand by skilled, experienced craftsmen.'

A number of notes and remarks in the catalogue offer further intriguing insights into the way in which the firm conducted its business. A picture of a large and efficient organisation emerges. Customers visiting the showrooms were assured of helpful attention, and those coming from a distance or spending a great deal of time in selecting their purchases were offered refreshment. But it was the clear intention of the high quality illustrations in the catalogue to make it possible to choose items and have them sent without the need for visiting the city at all if the client preferred. The details provided of delivery arrangements reveal a highly organised system; the firm's own horse-drawn vans made 'Twice Daily' rounds, delivering free to the West End, Chelsea, Pimlico, Kensington and Regent's Park. The City, the Docks (for shipping goods) and other areas of 'Town' were served 'Once Daily'. The suburbs, out to a radius of twelve miles, were covered by an arrangement with a firm of specialist carriers, Messrs. Carter, Patterson and Co's Conveyances, also free of charge; whilst greater distances were by arrangement. For deliveries to other parts of the country a no less efficient system obtained, whereby goods were sent by rail in Hampton's own 'Pantechnicon Vans' or in the railways companies' own vans. 'If required' it was offered 'we send at a Moderate Charge an Experienced Man to meet the goods on arrival, to superintend the unloading and delivery'.

A further significant feature of the catalogue was a section which gave proposed selections of items intended to furnish fully, and down to the last minute requirement, a variety of different sorts of house. Examples ranged from a selection of furnishings and all the necessary domestic items for 'a House containing eight rooms' at £250, rising by stages to cover ten, twelve, fourteen, sixteen and eighteen-roomed residences; this last costing the not inconsiderable, but still keenly-priced sum of £2000. As a service for newly-wed couples or those intending to set up home in far-flung places, these specimen contents lists were doubtless of immense value. They draw upon items from every section of the catalogue and, naturally, give a highly valuable insight into the notions of the day concerning what was required to make an ordinary house comfortable and efficient. Compared with similar exercises undertaken in more recent times by furnishing firms such as Habitat, the Hampton's lists reveal a curious balance of prices, in many ways quite unlike those of today. In 1894 many relatively dull pieces of drawing room or dining-room furniture were costly when measured against the earnings of the day for the professional man and staggering when compared with the expectations of the artisan or workman; by contrast, and reversing the present situation, the entire contents of the kitchen and other service parts of the house, including a vast array of specialized items of equipment including ironmongery, tablewares and so forth, cost a relatively small proportion, around one tenth of the total expenditure.

It is a curious fact that today, interest in the workings of houses great and small has never been greater. Visitors to properties owned by the National Trust and other historic houses that are open to the public take tremendous delight in inspecting the kitchens and other 'below stairs' parts. By comparison, however, with the grander sort of house, relatively less is known about the domestic arrangements of small, ordinary houses for the simple reason that in more modest dwellings things have far less often survived untouched from an earlier period. Similarly, domestic life in the town-house or in the surburban villa of the turn of the century operated upon lines and traditions that have vanished far more completely than those of the country house. Again, therefore, Hampton's pages offer a remarkable insight into the detail of the ordinary domestic objects of the day. Of particular fascination are those pages which deal with the new gadgetry of the moment, and which reveal the old, such as gas and paraffin lamps alongside the, then, highly novel, electric lights. The extent to which the new technology at first borrowed the forms of the old, but rapidly went on to develop a visual language all of its own can readily be demonstrated by comparing the various types of standing lamp fitments and the changing shape and overall aesthetic of the wall-bracket light.

Other electric innovations included a motor-powered fan suitable for 'cooling Dining and Ball Rooms'; an expensive novelty at £9.15s. An electrically-heated 'apparatus' for curling tongs, an electric torch and a cigar-lighter, the latter being in an elaborately ornamented style and costing four guineas, all clearly demonstrate the extent to which such innovations were firmly in the luxury goods bracket at this date. Similarly, the various fittings and switches for fully installed electric lighting were relatively costly. A wealth of curious and unfamiliar forms is revealed, including elaborate ceiling rose fittings, elegant switches with fluted and other patterns stamped into their brass covers, and extraordinary cut-glass ornamental light bulbs.

The early sanitary wares and other bathroom and kitchen fittings have a similar appeal, providing excellent documentary evidence of aspects of the ordinary house that have for the most part completely disappeared in the course of modernisation. In fact, for those in search of precise information about all manner of details of the domestic scene in the 1890s the Hampton's catalogue is an invaluable resource, revealing many aspects of the late Victorian home which would be otherwise extremely difficult to visualise or verify.

In describing the present catalogue, Hampton's manager wrote with not inconsiderable pride that, having 'determined to publish a book of designs...surpassing in every respect anything of the kind yet produced', he felt that the resulting volume 'may fairly be claimed to be, both as regards the artistic merit of its contents and as an example of the latest methods of photographic reproduction, unique and without a rival'. To some degree the publication of the catalogue in 1894 represented a high-water-mark of the firm's ambitions and achievement, but as a business Hampton's was to continue to flourish in Pall Mall East for another half a century.

Then during the Second World War the shop was hit by a succession of bombs. Five hits did considerable damage, but the sixth, a high-powered incendiary bomb which fell on one of the worst nights of the Blitz in November 1940, gutted the building and all but destroyed any prospect that the business could carry on. Photographs taken after that night show the entire block in a sorry state, every window in the area blown out and the streets full of rubble. Fortunately the pictures from the National Gallery next door had been removed to the safety of a deep mine in Wales at the outbreak of hostilities. After the war, shattered remains of the store formed just one of many inner-city bomb sites for which grandiose plans were hatched. Initially the Canadian government bought out the old Hampton's leases and freeholds at a time when proposals were afoot to create a magnificent group of colonial and Commonwealth High Commission buildings around Trafalgar Square. Already, however, the National Gallery had fixed their eye on what was always know as the Hampton site as the most suitable location for an extension. But it was to be another thirty years before the new Sainsbury Wing of the gallery finally opened its doors. Ironically, Hampton's, founded in 1830, just six years later than the establishment of the National Gallery, had already occupied its position for five years before Wilkinson's building was completed on Trafalgar Square. As neighbours for over a century, only the vagaries of bombing ended the life of one of London's major stores. Today, Hampton's monument lies, if you seek it, in these pages.

DESIGNS FOR FURNITURE AND DECORATIONS

FOR

COMPLETE HOUSE FURNISHING

BY

HAMPTON & SONS.

Illustrated with Fifty Collotype Reproductions of Artistic Interiors, in various styles, specially designed for this work; upwards of 2,000 Half-tone Blocks of Furniture Photographed from Stock, and many Coloured Illustrations of Carpets, Curtains, Linens, Blinds, China and Glass, etc.

PALL MALL EAST & COCKSPUR ST., LONDON, S.W.

ESTABLISHED 1830.

A FLEMISH RENAISSANCE HALL.

HAMPTON & SONS,

PALL MALL EAST, LONDON, S.W.

A DINING HALL IN THE ELIZABETHAN STYLE.

HAMPTON & SONS,

PALL MALL EAST, LONDON, S.W.

DINING ROOM IN THE STYLE OF THE ITALIAN RENAISSANCE.

HAMPTON & SONS,

PALL MALL EAST, LONDON, S.W.

A PLAIN MODERN DINING-ROOM.

HAMPTON & SONS,

PALL MALL EAST, LONDON, S.W.

AN INEXPENSIVE DINING ROOM.

HAMPTON & SONS,

PALL MALL EAST, LONDON, S.W.

A SMOKING ROOM, IN THE ORIENTAL STYLE.

HAMPTON & SONS,

PALL MALL EAST, LONDON, S.W.

A LIBRARY, IN THE ITALIAN RENAISSANCE STYLE.

HAMPTON & SONS,

PALL MALL EAST, LONDON, S.W.

A FITTED LIBRARY, IN THE QUEEN ANNE STYLE.

HAMPTON & SONS,

PALL MALL EAST, LONDON, S.W.

A MODERN LIBRARY.

HAMPTON & SONS,

PALL MALL EAST, LONDON, S.W.

A BILLIARD ROOM.

HAMPTON & SONS,

PALL MALL EAST, LONDON, S.W.

A QUEEN ANNE MORNING ROOM.

HAMPTON & SONS,

PALL MALL EAST, LONDON, S.W.

AN ALCOVE FITMENT.

Hampton & Sons,
PALL MALL EAST, LONDON, S.W.

A COSY CORNER.

A DRAWING-ROOM IN THE ADAMS' STYLE.

HAMPTON & SONS,

PALL MALL EAST, LONDON, S.W.

DRAWING-ROOM IN THE LOUIS XVI. STYLE.

HAMPTON & SONS,

PALL MALL EAST, LONDON, S.W.

DRAWING-ROOM IN THE LOUIS XV. STYLE.

HAMPTON & SONS,

PALL MALL EAST, LONDON, S.W.

A DRAWING ROOM IN THE CHIPPENDALE STYLE.

HAMPTON & SONS,

PALL MALL EAST, LONDON, S.W.

A BOUDOIR.

HAMPTON & SONS,

PALL MALL EAST, LONDON, S.W.

A DRAWING-ROOM INGLE NOOK.

HAMPTON & SONS,

PALL MALL EAST, LONDON, S.W.

TWO QUEEN ANNE CHIMNEY PIECES.

HAMPTON & SONS,

PALL MALL EAST, LONDON, S.W.

LOUIS XV. STYLE.

COSY CORNERS.

LOUIS XVI. STYLE.

HAMPTON & SONS,

PALL MALL EAST, LONDON, S.W.

AN INGLE NOOK.

HAMPTON & SONS,

PALL MALL EAST, LONDON, S.W.

A BEDROOM, WITH RICHLY INLAID FURNITURE.

HAMPTON & SONS,

PALL MALL EAST, LONDON, S.W.

ELEVATIONS AND PLAN OF A
FITTED & FURNISHED BEDROOM.

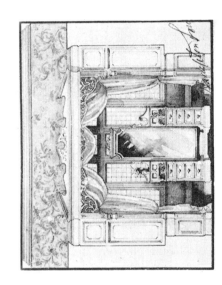

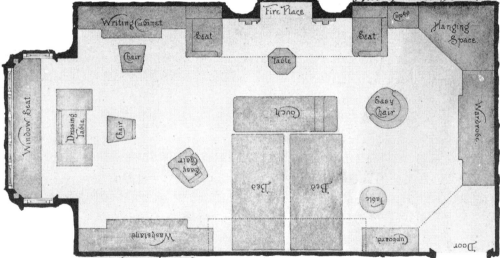

Writing Cabinet

Fire Place

Cup^d

Hanging Space.

Seat

Seat

Chair

Table

Window Seat.

Dressing Table

Chair

Couch

Easy Chair

Easy Chair

Bed

Bed

Table

Wardrobe.

Washstand

Cupboard

Door

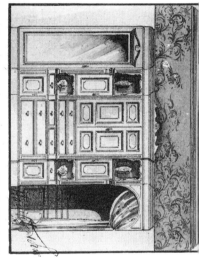

HAMPTON & SONS,
PALL MALL EAST, LONDON, S.W.

A FITTED BED ROOM.

HAMPTON & SONS,

PALL MALL EAST, LONDON, S.W.

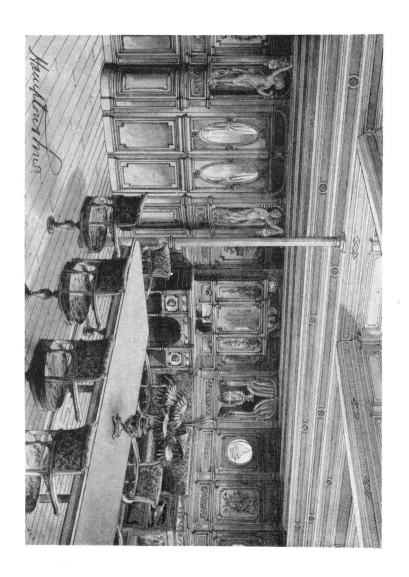

A YACHT SALOON.

HAMPTON & SONS,

PALL MALL EAST, LONDON, S.W.

A MODERN BATH-ROOM IN THE POMPEIAN STYLE.

HAMPTON & SONS,

PALL MALL EAST, LONDON, S.W.

Hampton & Sons' Valve Closets & Automatic Cisterns.

S 18.

"'Compound" Wash-down Closet. Recommended. £2 15s.

S 19.

The " Warwick " Closet, with Lead Trap.
Recommended as a good Sanitary Fitting   £1 8s. 6d.

S 20.

"' Simplicitas " Wash-down Closet and Trap, in
one piece of Earthenware, clean and sanitary, as shown above and fitted in Show
Rooms   ...   .   £2 5s.

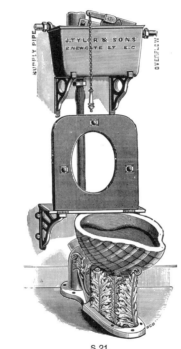

S 21.

The " Compound " Wash-down Closet, complete,
with Flushing Cistern and Mahogany Seat, &c.   £6 10s.

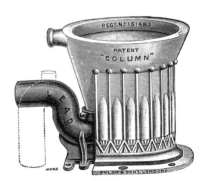

S 22.

" Column " Pedestal Closet, with Lead Trap.
Recommended as a good Sanitary Fitting,
connection to Soil Pipe being made with a
Wiped Joint, with good Flushing facilities,
as shown above and fitted in Show Rooms...   £2 5s.

HAMPTON & SONS, PALL MALL EAST AND COCKSPUR STREET, LONDON, S.W.

ALL GOODS CARRIAGE PAID—SEE PREFACE.

Hampton & Sons' Improved Tip-up Lavatories.

S 35.

In Polished Walnut, Veined Marble Top, 16 in. White and Gold Tip-up Basin, Soap and Brush Trays, Hot and Cold Valves, Shampoo, Douche, and Spray Bracket, lower part enclosed with cupboards, as shown ... ... £25 10s.

S 36.

Polished Mahogany or Walnut Two-person Lavatory, fitted with White and Gold 14 in. Basins, Marble Top, Soap and Brush Trays, Hot and Cold Valves, lower part enclosed as shown ... £35.

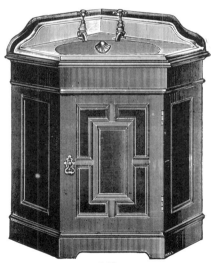

S 37.

Angle Cabinet Lavatory, in Polished Mahogany or Walnut, with Hot and Cold Taps, as shown ... ... £6 15s. 0d.
Plated fittings ... ... extra 4s. 6d.

HAMPTON & SONS, PALL MALL EAST AND COCKSPUR STREET, LONDON, S.W.

ALL GOODS CARRIAGE PAID—SEE PREFACE.

HAMPTON & SONS' IMPROVED CABINET & ROMAN BATHS.

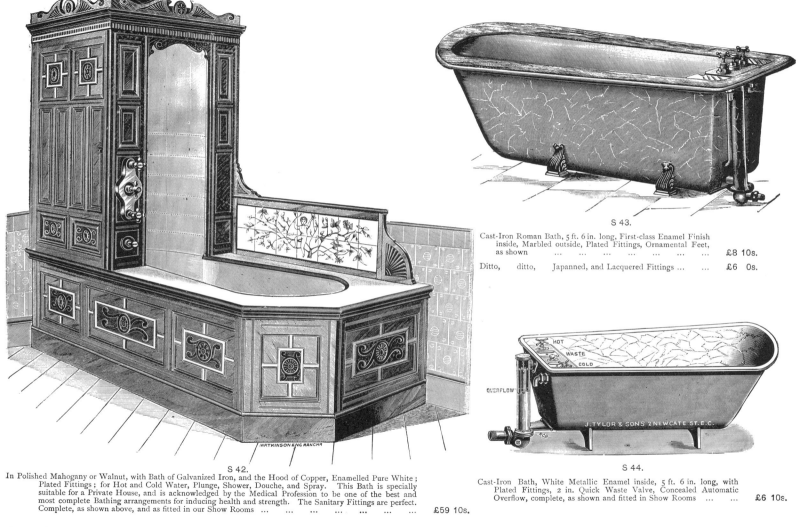

S 43.

Cast-Iron Roman Bath, 5 ft. 6 in. long, First-class Enamel Finish
inside, Marbled outside, Plated Fittings, Ornamental Feet,
as shown ... ... £8 10s.

Ditto, ditto, Japanned, and Lacquered Fittings ... ... £6 0s.

S 44.

Cast-Iron Bath, White Metallic Enamel inside, 5 ft. 6 in. long, with
Plated Fittings, 2 in. Quick Waste Valve, Concealed Automatic
Overflow, complete, as shown and fitted in Show Rooms ... ... £6 10s.

S 42.

In Polished Mahogany or Walnut, with Bath of Galvanized Iron, and the Hood of Copper, Enamelled Pure White;
Plated Fittings; for Hot and Cold Water, Plunge, Shower, Douche, and Spray. This Bath is specially
suitable for a Private House, and is acknowledged by the Medical Profession to be one of the best and
most complete Bathing arrangements for inducing health and strength. The Sanitary Fittings are perfect.
Complete, as shown above, and as fitted in our Show Rooms ... ... £59 10s.

HAMPTON & SONS, PALL MALL EAST AND COCKSPUR STREET, LONDON, S.W.

ALL GOODS CARRIAGE PAID—SEE PREFACE.

HAMPTON & SONS' ELECTRIC LIGHT FITTINGS.

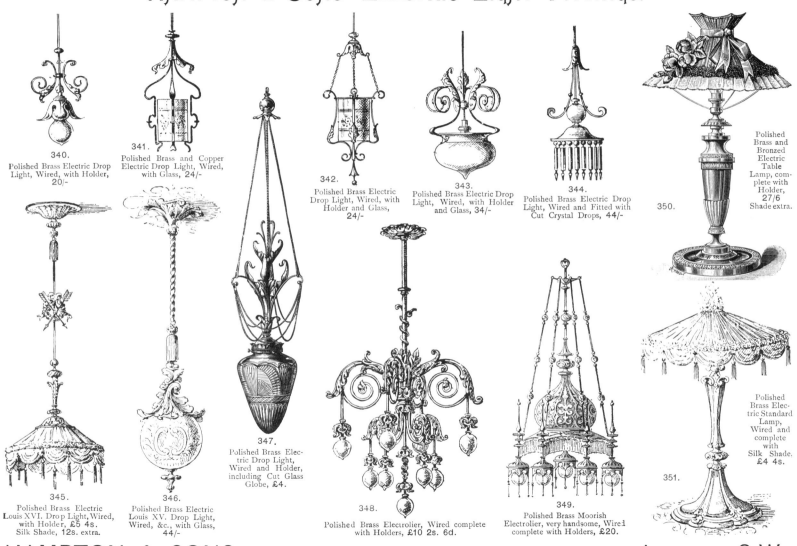

340.
Polished Brass Electric Drop Light, Wired, with Holder, 20/-

341.
Polished Brass and Copper Electric Drop Light, Wired, with Glass, 24/-

342.
Polished Brass Electric Drop Light, Wired, with Holder and Glass, 24/-

343.
Polished Brass Electric Drop Light, Wired, with Holder and Glass, 34/-

344.
Polished Brass Electric Drop Light, Wired and Fitted with Cut Crystal Drops, 44/-

350.
Polished Brass and Bronzed Electric Table Lamp, complete with Holder, 27/6 Shade extra.

345.
Polished Brass Electric Louis XVI. Drop Light, Wired, with Holder, £5 4s. Silk Shade, 12s. extra.

346.
Polished Brass Electric Louis XV. Drop Light, Wired, &c., with Glass, 44/-

347.
Polished Brass Electric Drop Light, Wired and Holder, including Cut Glass Globe, £4.

348.
Polished Brass Electrolier, Wired complete with Holders, £10 2s. 6d.

349.
Polished Brass Moorish Electrolier, very handsome, Wired complete with Holders, £20.

351.
Polished Brass Electric Standard Lamp, Wired and complete with Silk Shade, £4 4s.

HAMPTON & SONS, PALL MALL EAST AND COCKSPUR STREET, LONDON, S.W.

ALL GOODS CARRIAGE PAID—SEE PREFACE.

HAMPTON & SONS' LATEST ELECTRIC LIGHT NOVELTIES.

S 65.

⅛ H.-P. Motor, fitted with 12-in. Wing Fan, for cooling Dining and Ball Rooms, &c. ... ... £9 15s.

S 66.

The Electric Rapid Cooking Apparatus, as shown ; most useful for Domestic Purposes ... ... £4 10s.

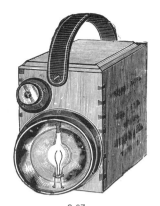

S 67.

Portable Electric Light, in Case, with Battery complete ; very useful to travellers ... ... £3 18s. 6d.

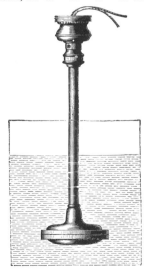

S 68.

The Electric Water Heater ; for heating water quickly... ... ... £2.

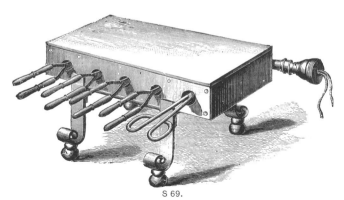

S 69.

Electric Apparatus for Heating Curling Irons, &c., can be had in various sizes as required. ... ... Prices on application according to requirements.

S 70.

Electric Cigar Lighter, always ready for use and very convenient for Smoking Room ... ... £4 4s.

HAMPTON & SONS, PALL MALL EAST AND COCKSPUR STREET, LONDON, S.W.

ALL GOODS CARRIAGE PAID—SEE PREFACE.

HAMPTON & SONS' MATS.

No. 222.—FANCY IMPERIAL.

IMPERIAL, with Worsted Border and Monogram.

No. 224.—FANCY IMPERIAL.

FIBRE BRUSH, with Colored Border and Device.

No. 223.—FANCY IMPERIAL.

PLAIN FIBRE BRUSH, with Coat of Arms.

No. 225.—FANCY BRUSH.

No. 221.—FANCY IMPERIAL, Lettered.

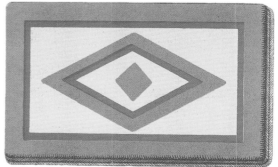

No. 226.—FANCY BRUSH.

HAMPTON & SONS, Pall Mall East, and Cockspur Street, Charing Cross, London, s.w.

HAMPTON & SONS' Inside Blinds.

L7.—ART PRINTED, 3ft. 6in. × 6ft., 7/9.
EXCLUSIVE OF ROLLER.

L8.—RESEDA DAMASK, 3ft. 6in. × 6ft., 11/9.
EXCLUSIVE OF ROLLER.

L9.—PALE TERRA-COTTA DAMASK, 3ft. 6in. × 6ft., 13/6.
EXCLUSIVE OF ROLLER.

K10.—RED SILK FESTOON. from 1 6 per square foot,
in any shade.

L11.—BUFF DUCHESSE, 3ft. 6in. × 6ft., 14/6.
EXCLUSIVE OF ROLLER.

C12.—7d. to 9d. per square foot, painted any shade,
fluted and varnished, super webs and cords.
Best quality do., with worsted webs, 10d. per square foot.
Patent check action, 1d. per square foot extra.
Blinds measuring less than 16 square feet charged as 16 feet.
Old Venetian Blinds repaired and Re-Taped with new
cords from 4d. per square foot.

HAMPTON & SONS, Pall Mall East, London, S.W.

K 18.—ORIENTAL DESIGN. Bordered and Fringed.
3½ yards long, 13/9 per pair.
ALSO MADE IN BLUE AND CAMEL GROUNDS.

K 19.—ORIENTAL DESIGN. Reversible Tapestry, Fringed at Base.
3½ yards long, 14/9 per pair.
ALSO MADE IN RED AND CAMEL GROUNDS.

HAMPTON & SONS, Pall Mall East, and Cockspur Street, Charing Cross, London, s.w.

K 24.—DJIJIM.

K 25.—KHELIM.

HAMPTON & SONS, Pall Mall East, and Cockspur Street, Charing Cross, London, S.W.

K 40.—DRAPED DRESSING TABLE.

K 41.—DRAPED MANTEL AND OVERMANTEL.

HAMPTON & SONS, Pall Mall East and Cockspur Street, Charing Cross, London, S.W.

Hampton & Sons' Designs for Draperies.

K 42.—SIDE OF BEDROOM WITH DRAPED AND CANOPIED FRENCH BEDSTEAD.

HAMPTON & SONS, Pall Mall East, and Cockspur Street, Charing Cross, London, S.W.

HAMPTON & SONS' TEA SERVICES, ETC.

G. 13.
Tea Service, 40 pieces ... £1 18 6
Breakfast ,, 51 ,, ... 3 15 6

G. 14.
Tea Service for 12 persons £1 18 6

G. 15.
Tea Service for 12 persons ... £1 12 3
Breakfast ,, ,, ... 3 17 10

G. 16.
Tea Service for 12 persons ... £3 14 0

G. 17.
Tea Service for 12 persons ... £1 8 9
Breakfast ,, ,, ... 3 10 0

G. 18.
Dessert Service for 12 persons ... £3 9 6

G. 19.
Dessert Service for 12 persons ... £4 1 3

G. 20.
Dessert Service for 12 persons ... £4 2 6

For enumeration of pieces comprising services, see opposite page.

G. 21.
Dessert Service for 12 persons ... £2 5 0

G. 22.
Dessert Service for 12 persons ... £5 11 0

G. 23.
Dinner Service for 12 persons ... £4 4 6

G. 24.
Dinner Service for 12 persons ... £5 3 9

G. 25. Plain White Dinner Service for 12 persons, with Solid Gilt Handles, £3 19 0

G. 26.
Dinner Service for 12 persons ... £8 7 9

G. 27.
Dinner Service for 12 persons ... £4 4 6

G. 28. Single Set, 5 pieces ... £1 10 0
Double ,, 11 ,, ... 3 7 0

G. 29. Single Set, 5 pieces ... £1 17 6
Double ,, 11 ,, ... 4 3 9

ATKINSON BROTHERS,
LITHOGRAPHERS,
ORIEL WORKS, HANLEY, ENGLAND.

G. 30. Single Set ... £0 10 0
Double ,, ... 1 2 3

G. 31. Single Set ... £1 15 0
Double ,, ... 3 18 2

HAMPTON & SONS, PALL MALL EAST & COCKSPUR STREET, CHARING CROSS, LONDON, S.W.

HAMPTON & SONS' DESSERT SERVICES, ETC.

G. 48.
Dessert Service for 12 persons ... £7 5 9

G. 49.
Dessert Service for 12 persons ... £6 11 3

G. 50.
Dessert Service for 12 persons ... £3 6 9

G. 51.
Dessert Service for 12 persons ... £4 4 6

G. 52.
Dessert Service for 12 persons ... £4 2

G. 53.
Dessert Service for 12 persons
£4 3 6

G. 54.
Tea Set for 12 persons ... £1 10 9
Breakfast Set for 6 persons ... 1 8 0

G. 55. Four o'clock Tea Set ... £2 5 0

For enumeration
of pieces
comprising services,
see
opposite page.

G. 56.
Tea Set for 12 persons ... £2 1 6
Breakfast Set ,, ... 3 15 9

G. 57.
Dessert Service for 12 persons
£4 7 6

G. 58.
Dessert Service for 12 persons
£3 5 0

G. 59.
Tea Set for 12 persons ... £1 13 6
Breakfast Set ,, ... 3 6 6

G. 60.
Tea Set for 12 persons ... £2 2 9
Breakfast Set ,, ... 3 19 9

G. 61.
Dessert Service for 12 persons
£3 16 0

G. 62.
Dessert Service for 12 persons
£1 12 6

G. 63.
Tea Set for 12 persons ... £3 17 6

G. 64.
Toilet Table Set ... £2 7 6

G. 65.
Tea Set for 12 persons ... £1 16 0
Breakfast Set ,, ... 3 9 3

G. 66.
Dessert Service for 12 persons
£3 5 9

ATKINSON BROTHERS, LITHOGRAPHERS, ORIEL WORKS, HANLEY, ENGLAND.

HAMPTON & SONS, PALL MALL EAST & COCKSPUR STREET, CHARING CROSS, LONDON, S.W.

HAMPTON & SONS' FRIEZES.

Friezes, Ceiling Panels and Borders, in Fibrous Plaster, Tynecastle Tapestry, Vellum, &c.

D 11. *Canvas Plaster.*

D 12. *Ceiling Panels, ¾-in. in Relief.*

D 13. *Canvas Plaster.*

D 14. *8¼-in. deep.*

D 15. *Vintage Frieze, in Embossed Canvas, 11-ft. 4-in. long.   Made in Panels 2-ft. 10-in. each.*

D 16. *8¼-in. deep.*

D 17. *½-in. in Relief.*

D 18. *Ceiling Panel 7-16th-in. in Relief.*

D 19. *⅞-in. in Relief.*

ANY OF THE ABOVE CAN BE SUPPLIED PLAIN FOR DISTEMPERING OR PAINTING, OR DECORATED IN COLORS READY FOR FIXING.

HAMPTON & SONS,

PALL MALL EAST AND COCKSPUR STREET, CHARING CROSS, LONDON, S.W.

HAMPTON & SONS' FRIEZES.

FRIEZES IN HIGH RELIEF IN ANAGLYPTA LEATHER PAPER, EMBOSSED CANVAS, AND IN SPECIALLY PREPARED MATERIALS, MODELLED IN ARTISTIC DESIGNS.

D 20. *Embossed Leather Paper.*

D 21. *Embossed Leather Paper.*

D 22. *Embossed Leather Paper.*

D 23. *Embossed Canvas.*

HAMPTON & SONS,

PALL MALL EAST AND COCKSPUR STREET, CHARING CROSS, LONDON, S.W.

D 28. *Price in Colors, 4s. per Piece.*
Frieze, from 1s. per yard.

D 29. *Price in Colors, from 3s. 6d. per Piece.*

D 30. *Price in Colors, 5s. 6d. per Piece.*

HAMPTON & SONS' DECORATIONS.

SCHEMES OF COLOUR AND ESTIMATES FOR THESE DECORATIONS MAY BE HAD ON APPLICATION.

Treatment No. 4.

Treatment No. 5.

Treatment No. 6.

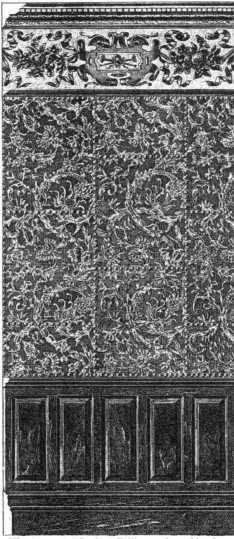

The Dado in Modelled Canvas in high relief.
The filling, embossed vellum.

Wood-panelled Dado. Filling, embossed leather
in studded panels. Hand-painted Frieze.

Printed Tapestry, hanging from beneath shelf.
Frieze in leather paper.

HAMPTON & SONS,

PALL MALL EAST AND COCKSPUR STREET, CHARING CROSS, LONDON, S.W.

D 36. *Pine, primed for painting, 10s. 6d.*

D 39. *Pine, primed for painting ...   ... 35s.*
Oak, Walnut, or Mahogany   ... 65s.

D 42. *Pine, primed for painting, 55s.*

D 37. *Pine, primed for painting, 22s. 6d.*

D 40. *Pine, primed for painting, 37s. 6d.*

D 43. *Pine, with carved or cartoon-pierre enrich-*
ment, primed for painting.

D 38. *Pine, primed for painting   ... 25s.*
Oak, Walnut, or Mahogany ... 47s. 6d.

D 41. *Pine, primed for painting ...   ... 45s.*
Oak, Walnut, or Mahogany   ... 85s.

D 44. *Pine, carved or cartoon-pierre for painting.*

HAMPTON & SONS,

PALL MALL EAST AND COCKSPUR STREET, CHARING CROSS, LONDON, S.W.

HAMPTON & SONS' DOORS AND OVERDOORS.

JOINERY WORK OF EVERY DESCRIPTION AT MODERATE PRICES.   DESIGNS AND ESTIMATES SUBMITTED.

DESIGNS FOR DOORS AND OVERDOORS EXECUTED IN HARD WOOD BY CABINETMAKERS; ALSO MADE IN PINE, WITH CARTOON-PIERRE ENRICHMENTS, FOR PAINTING.
ARCHITECTS' DESIGNS CAREFULLY EXECUTED.

HAMPTON & SONS,

PALL MALL EAST AND COCKSPUR STREET, CHARING CROSS, LONDON, S.W.

No. D76.

Carved & Fumigated oak Chimney-piece & Overmantel		£19.10.0.
Black Abbotsford Grate fitted with tiles,	- from	3.13.6.
Tile Hearth to match,	- ,,	1. 1.0.
Wrought iron Curb,	,,	5.15.0.
A pair of wrought iron Standards, with poker and tongs	,,	4. 5.0.

No. D77.

Walnut Chimney-piece and Overmantel	- -	£22.10.0.
Black and brass Abbotsford Grate	- from	5.10.0.
Tile Hearth to suit	,,	0.18.6.
Black and brass Curb	,,	2. 7.6.

No. D71.
White Chimney-piece and Overmantel, - - - - £24. 0. 0.
Brass Dog Grate, 10.10.0. Curb - - - - *from* 5.15.0.

No. D72.
White Chimney-piece and Overmantel, - - - - £35. 0. 0.
Steel Grate, - - - - - - - *from* 18. 8. 0.
Embossed Brass Curb, 5.15.0. Rests - - - - ,, 3. 5. 0.

HAMPTON & SONS,
PALL MALL EAST AND COCKSPUR STREET, CHARING CROSS, LONDON, S.W.
ALL GOODS CARRIAGE PAID—SEE PREFACE.
EVERY ARTICLE IN CATALOGUE PHOTOGRAPHED FROM STOCK.

HAMPTON & SONS' Outside Blinds.

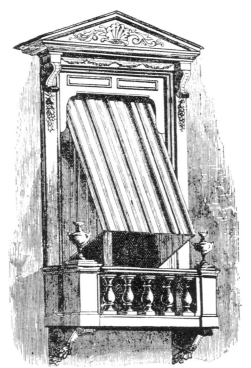

C 1.

CANALETTI BLIND.
ON SPRING ROLLERS.

In Best Blue and White Barnsley Tick, **1/7** per square foot.
In Best Fancy Striped „ „ **1/9** „ „

C 2.

FLORENTINE BLIND.

In Best Blue and White Barnsley Tick, **1/8½** per square foot.
In Best Fancy Striped „ „ **1/11** „ „

C 3.

SPANISH BLIND.

In Best Blue and White Barnsley Tick, **2/2** per square foot.
In Best Fancy Striped „ „ **2/4** „ „

Blinds containing less than 20 square feet charged as 20 feet.

Experienced men sent to take instructions and measurements, also to submit patterns and advise as to what Blinds would be most suitable.

Estimates for Door, Verandah, and Balcony, Conservatory Blinds and Awnings upon application, also for Renewing Old Blinds, Repairing Boxes, &c.

HAMPTON & SONS, Pall Mall East, and Cockspur Street, Charing Cross, London, S.W.

HAMPTON & SONS' Outside Blinds.

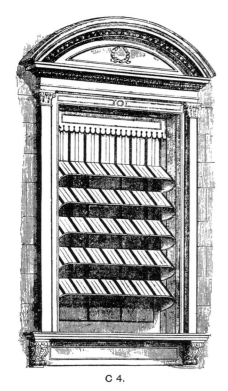

C 4.	C 5.	C 6.

HELIOSCENE BLIND.

In Best Blue and White Barnsley Tick, **2/6** per square foot.
In Best Fancy Striped ,, ,, **2/9** ,, ,,

ORIENTAL BLIND.

In Best Blue and White Barnsley Tick, **2/7** per square foot.
In Best Fancy Striped ,, ,, **2/9** ,, ,,

OUTSIDE SHUTTER BLINDS.

Painted any color... ... ... **3/3** per square foot.
Painted any color, to slide with wrought-
iron Rails and moulded Cornices ... **3/9** ,, ,,

Blinds containing less than 20 square feet charged as 20 feet.

Experienced men sent to take instructions and measurements, also to submit patterns and Estimates for Door, Verandah, and Balcony, Conservatory Blinds and Awnings, and for Renewing Old Blinds, Repairing Boxes, &c., upon application.

HAMPTON & SONS, Pall Mall East, and Cockspur Street, Charing Cross, London, S.W.

HAMPTON & SONS' CHENILLE CURTAINS.

K 22.—CHENILLE CURTAINS.

K 23.—CHENILLE—Special Design.

HAMPTON & SONS, Pall Mall East, and Cockspur Street, Charing Cross, London, s.w.

HAMPTON & SONS' DESIGNS FOR DRAPERIES.

K **40.**—DRAPED DRESSING TABLE.

K **41.**—DRAPED MANTEL AND OVERMANTEL.

HAMPTON & SONS, Pall Mall East and Cockspur Street, Charing Cross, London, S.W.

K **30.**—DESIGN FOR DRAPING A BAY WINDOW.

HAMPTON & SONS, Pall Mall East, and Cockspur Street, Charing Cross, London, s.w.

Hampton & Sons' Designs for Pelmets and Draperies.

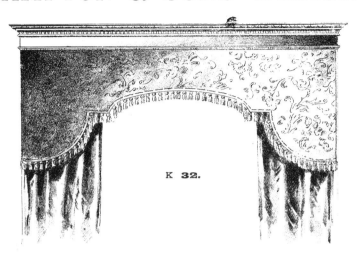

K 32.

K 33.

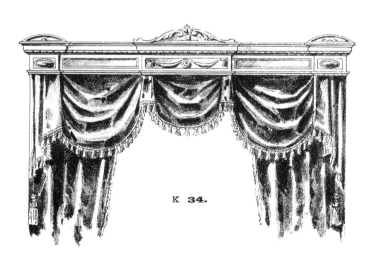

K 34.

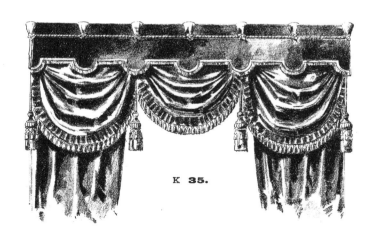

K 35.

HAMPTON & SONS, Pall Mall East, and Cockspur Street, Charing Cross, London, s.w.

Hampton & Sons' Designs for Draperies.

K **43.**—BEDSTEAD FOOTEND.

K **44.**—BEDSTEAD FOOTEND.

K **45.**—PIANO BACK.

K **46.**—PIANO BACK.

HAMPTON & SONS, Pall Mall East, and Cockspur Street, Charing Cross, London, S.W.

L **47.**—63 inches × 3½ yards, 7/9.   63 inches × 4 yards, 8/9 per pair.

L **48.**—63 inches × 3½ yards, 10/6.   63 inches × 4 yards, 11/9.   63 inches × 4½ yards, 13/6 per pair.

HAMPTON & SONS, Pall Mall East, and Cockspur Street, Charing Cross, London, S.W.

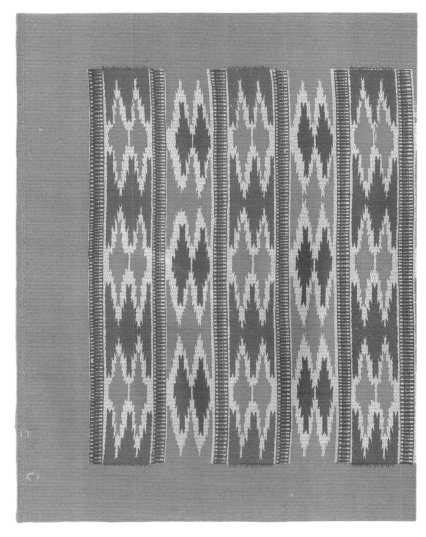

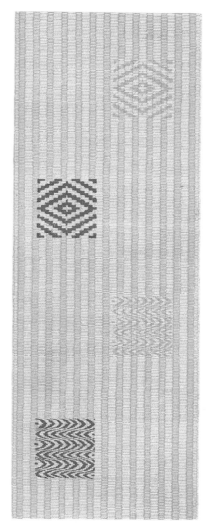

THE MUNG MATTING—Seamless.

INSERTED JAPANESE.

HAMPTON & SONS, Pall Mall East, and Cockspur Street, Charing Cross, London, s.w.

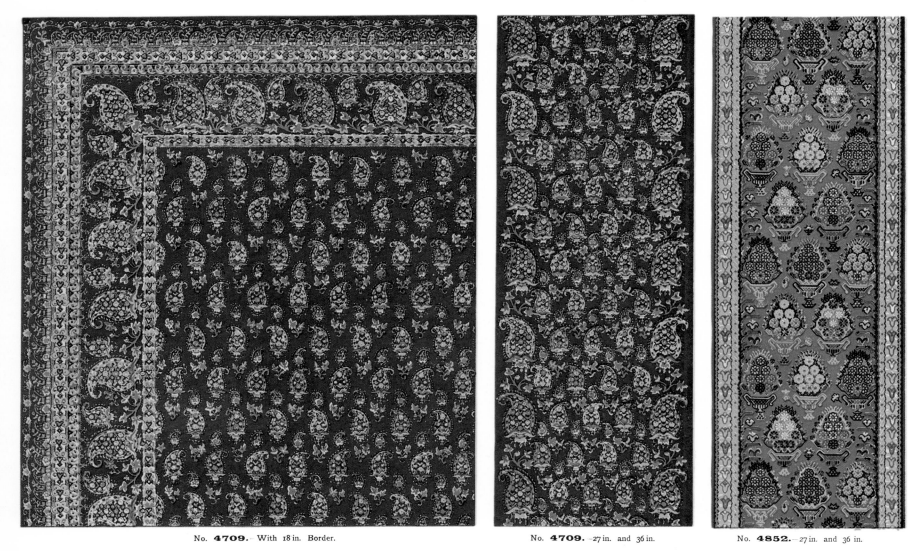

No. **4709.** With 18 in. Border.   No. **4709.** —27 in. and 36 in.   No. **4852.** —27 in. and 36 in.

HAMPTON & SONS, Pall Mall East, and Cockspur Street, Charing Cross, London, s.w.

HAMPTON & SONS' SEAMLESS AXMINSTER CARPETS.

RED GROUND. CAMEL GROUND. BLUE GROUND.

No. **8348.**

HAMPTON & SONS, Pall Mall East, and Cockspur Street, Charing Cross, London, S.W.

INDIAN DESIGN.
All sizes in stock, various colored grounds.

STAIR CARPETING in various widths.
Billiard Surrounds to match.

HAMPTON & SONS, Pall Mall East, and Cockspur Street, Charing Cross, London, S.W.

For Quotations see page 84.

All Sizes in Stock.

STAIR CARPETING in various widths.
Billiard Surrounds to match.

HAMPTON & SONS, Pall Mall East, and Cockspur Street, Charing Cross, London, S.W.

HAMPTON & SONS' KIDDERMINSTER CARPETS.

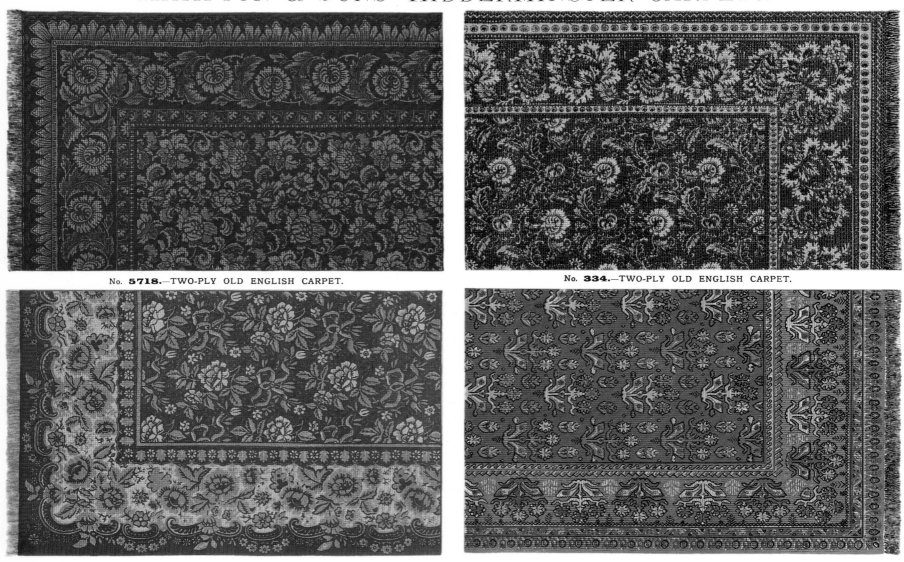

No. **5718.**—TWO-PLY OLD ENGLISH CARPET.

No. **334.**—TWO-PLY OLD ENGLISH CARPET.

No. **5220.**—BLUE THREE-PLY OLD ENGLISH CARPET.

No. **2001.**—ISTAKAHN CARPET.

HAMPTON & SONS, Pall Mall East, and Cockspur Street, Charing Cross, London, s.w.

No. 24.

Oak Monks' Bench, Chest, and Table, combined,—

Richly Carved, with Armorial Bearings and Motto,	3 ft. 6 in.,	£7.7.0.
	4 ft.	£8.8.0.
With Richly Carved Panels, but without Armorial	3 ft.	£5.15.0.
Bearings and Motto,	3 ft. 6 in.,	£6.6.0.

No. 25.
4 ft. 6 in. Old Oak Carved Chest.
£3.18.6.

No. 24, as Table.

No. 26.
4 ft. 6 in. Fumed Oak Carved Hall Settle and Chest.
£15.15.0.

No. 27.
Carved Dark Oak Arm Chair
£3.18.6.

No. 28.
5 ft. Fumed Oak Hall Settle, with Rug Box and richly Carved Frieze.—£13.10.0.

THESE ARE MADE IN OAK, WALNUT, AND MAHOGANY,

No. 29.
Umbrella Stand,
13s. 6d.

No. 30.
Umbrella Stand,
£1.16.6.

No. 33.
2 ft. Hall Stand, with
Bevelled Plate, £2.0.0.

No. 31.
Umbrella
Stand,
9s. 6d.

No. 34.
4 ft. Hall Stand, with Bevelled Plate.
£8.15.0.

No. 32. Corner
Umbrella Stand,
15s. 9d.

No. 35
2 ft. Hall Stand, with Brush
Drawer and Bevelled Plate.
£3.3.0.

HAMPTON & SONS,
PALL MALL EAST AND COCKSPUR STREET, CHARING CROSS, LONDON, S.W.

CARVED HALL FURNITURE.
MADE IN OAK AND WALNUT.

No. 73.—4 ft. 6 in.—£12.15.0.

No. 74.—£17.10.0.

No. 75.—5 ft.—£11.10.0.

No. 76.—5 ft.—£23.10.0.

No. 77.—3 ft. 3 in.—£5.15.0.

No. 78.—4 ft.—£15.15.0.

HAMPTON & SONS,
PALL MALL EAST AND COCKSPUR STREET, CHARING CROSS, LONDON, S.W.

THESE ARE MADE IN SOLID OAK, WALNUT, AND MAHOGANY.

No 89.
Superior stuffed back Chair, in best Morocco. 55s.

No. 90.
Heavy Oak stuffed back Chair. 58s. 6d.

No. 91.
Carved Oak Chair, in stamped Morocco or Hide. 72s. 6d.

No. 92.
Heavy well-made carved stuffed back Chair. 78s. 6d.

No. 93.
Pollard or fumed Oak Chair, in best Morocco. 78s. 6d.

No. 94. *Very large, massive, carved stuffed back Chair, in best Morocco, and large bronze nails.* £4.15.0.

No. 95. *Handsome carved stuffed back Chair, in Pig-skin.* £5.5.0.

No. 96. *High-back Elizabethan finely carved Oak Chair, in best Morocco or embossed Velvet.* £5.5.0.

No. 97. *High-back Queen Anne Chair, in embossed Velvet.* 57s. 6d.

No. 98. *Large richly carved Queen Anne Chair, with loose seat, covered in embossed Morocco or Velvet.* £5.15.0.

No. 115. *Low-back carved Dining Chair, to be placed alternately at the table with No. 115ᴬ in figured velvet.* 72s. 6d.

No. 115ᴬ *High-back Dining Chair, to be placed alternately with No. 115, in figured velvet.* 78s. 6d.

No. 116. *Arm Chair to match Nos. 115 and 115ᴬ* £5.10.0.

No. 117. *Finely carved Oak High-back Chair, in stamped hide.* 98s. 6d.

No. 118. *Well carved High-back Oak Chair, in embossed leather.* £5.5.0.

No. 119. *Carved Oak Chair, in frieze velvet.* 52s. 6d.

No. 120. *Carved Oak High-back Chair, in frieze velvet or morocco,* 57s. 6d. *In leather,* 50s. 0d.

No. 121. *Arm Chair.* £5.10.0.

HAMPTON & SONS,
PALL MALL EAST AND COCKSPUR STREET, CHARING CROSS, LONDON, S.W.

No. 123ᴬ.   No. 123.   No. 123ᴮ

No. 123ᶜ

Solid Oak, Walnut, or Mahogany Dining-Room Suite, consisting of 6 Small Chairs, 2 Easy Chairs, and a Couch, covered—In stamped morocco, **21** *Guineas.*
In saddle-bags, - **18** *Guineas.*

No. 125. *Heavy, fumed Oak, carved high-back Chair, in hide or best morocco* 78s 6d.

No. 125ᴬ *Carving Chair to match No.125.* £6.10.0.

No. 125ᴮ. *Arm Chair to match.* £8.10.0.

No. 125ᶜ *2nd Arm Chair to match No. 125.* £8.15.0.

No. 126ᴮ *Arm Chair to match.* £9.15.0.

No. 126ᴬ *Carving Arm Chair to match No. 126.* £6.10.0.

No. 126. *Heavy Fumed and carved Oak high-back Chair, in hide or best morocco.* 78s. 6d.

No. 127. *Fumed Oak, finely carved Arm Chair, in pigskin or best morocco.* £10.15.0

HAMPTON & SONS,
PALL MALL EAST ᴀɴᴅ COCKSPUR STREET, CHARING CROSS, LONDON, S.W.

No. 128.
£5.10.0.

No. 129.
£6.15.0.

No. 130.
£7.10.0.

No. 131.
£7.15.0.

No. 132.
Large, deep-seat Chair, stuffed best hair.
£8.15.0.

No. 133.
Very large, deep-seated Chair, stuffed best
hair.   **£9.15.0.**

HAMPTON & SONS,
PALL MALL EAST AND COCKSPUR STREET, CHARING CROSS, LONDON, S.W.

No. 134. In oak or walnut.
3 ft. 6 in. £2.5.0. 4 ft. £3.0.0.

No. 135. In oak or walnut, with superior mouldings.
3 ft. 6 in. £3.12.6 4 ft. £4.2.6.

No. 136. In oak, walnut, or mahogany, well made, superior finish. 3 ft. 6 in. £4.18.6 4 ft. £5.15.0.

No. 137. In oak or walnut, fitted with drawer, and cupboard with carved panel.
4 ft. 6 in. £5.7.6. 4 ft. £6.10.0.

No. 138. In oak, walnut, or mahogany, with carved back, and two drawers.
3 ft. 6 in. £5.10.0. 4 ft. £6.15.0.

No. 139. In mahogany, oak, or walnut, with carved columns, fine mouldings, best manufacture throughout.
4 ft. wide by 1 ft. 9 in. deep £8.10.0.
4 ft. 6 in. wide by 2 ft. deep £9.15.0.

No. 149.

Circular Dining Table, with extending screw, superior make, with legs within frame.

    4 ft. × 6 ft. £6.0.0.   4 ft. × 8 ft. £7.15.0.

Best make, with legs framed in frieze, as shown.

    4 ft. × 8 ft. £10.0.0.   4 ft. 3 in. × 10 ft. £13.10.0.

        4 ft. 6 in. × 12 ft. £16.15.0.

No. 150.

Dining Table, with elliptic ends, best make and superior finish, massive carved legs, in solid oak, walnut, or mahogany.

    4 ft.   × 8 ft. £10. 5.0.   4 ft. 6 in. × 10 ft. £13.10.0.

    4 ft. 3 in. × 9 ft. 11.10.0.   4 ft. 6 in. × 12 ft. 16.15.0.

No. 151.

Handsome Dining Table, with massive carved legs, best workmanship and finish throughout. In solid oak, walnut, or mahogany.

    4 ft. 6 in. × 12 ft. £18.15.0.   *5 ft.   × 18 ft. £30.15.0.

    *5 ft.   × 15 ft. 25.15.0.   *5 ft. 6 in. × 20 ft. 37.15.0.

No. 152. Jacobean finely carved Table, of best manufacture, with extending screws, constructed to hold all leaves not in use.

    4 ft.   × 8 ft. £11.10.0.   4 ft. 6 in. × 12 ft. £17.10.0.

    4 ft. 3 in. × 10 ft. 14.10.0.   *4 ft. 6 in. × 14 ft. 21.10.0.

Antique carved oak table, with carved moulding round top.

    4 ft.   × 8 ft. £9.9.0.   4 ft. 6 in. × 10 ft. £11.15.0.

* With extra carved leg in centre.

No. 165.

*Superior Sideboard of best manufacture, in Fumed Oak, Walnut, or Mahogany,
Richly Carved, and of fine finish throughout.*

6ft. 6in. wide.　35 Guineas.

No. 166.

*Superior Sideboard, of best manufacture, with finely Carved Frieze, Cornice
and Pediment supported by Carved Columns.*

6ft. 6in. wide.　35 Guineas.

HAMPTON & SONS,
PALL MALL EAST AND COCKSPUR STREET, CHARING CROSS, LONDON, S.W.

No. 175.
Carved Oak or Walnut
Pedestal.   **£4.15.0.**

No. 176.   Jacobean richly carved Old Oak Sideboard, Hampton & Sons' Regis-
tered Design, having Cellarets in Cupboards, as shown, instead of in the lower
part, the Decanters, &c. being thus within easy reach without stooping.
6ft. 6in.   **£39.10.0.**

No. 177.
Old carved Upright Eight-
day Clock.   **£11.10.0.**

HAMPTON & SONS,
PALL MALL EAST AND COCKSPUR STREET, CHARING CROSS, LONDON, S.W.

No. 178.

Old Mahogany inlaid Sheraton Sideboard, with serpentine front, long centre Drawer, with Cupboard on right hand side and fitted Cellaret Drawer at left side, brass lion's-head-with-ring handles, handsome enriched brass rail back with curtain, complete. 6ft. £22.10.0.

No. 179.

Old Mahogany inlaid Sheraton Sideboard, with shaped projecting front, drawers fitted with Cellaret, oval bevelled Glass above shelf in back. 6ft. 30 Guineas.

HAMPTON & SONS,
PALL MALL EAST AND COCKSPUR STREET, CHARING CROSS, LONDON, S.W.

No. 192.	No. 193.	No. 194.	No. 195.	No. 196.
Stained oak, walnut, or mahogany wood-seat Chair. **10s. 6d.**	*Stained oak, walnut, or mahogany wood-seat Chair.* **15s. 9d.**	*Stained oak, walnut, or dark mahogany wood-seat Chair.* **21s.**	*Stained oak, walnut, or dark mahogany wood-seat Chair.* **22s. 6d.**	*Dark mahogany wood-seat Chair,* **27s. 6d.**

No. 197.	No. 198.	No. 199.	No. 200.	No. 201.
Oak, walnut, or mahogany cane-seat chair. **24s. 30s.** *Wood-seat do.* **38s. 6d.**	*Oak, walnut, or mahogany cane-seat revolving Chair.* **30s. 38s. 6d.** *Wood-seat do.* **45s.**	*Oak, walnut, or mahogany, wood, deep-seated revolving Chair.* **42s.** *With cane seat,* **35s.**	*Superior well-finished revolving Chair, in oak, walnut, or mahogany, wood seat,* **55s**, *cane seat,* **47s.6d.**	*Superior well-finished revolving Chair, in oak, walnut, or mahogany, wood seat,* **72s.6d.**, *cane seat,* **65s.**

HAMPTON & SONS,

PALL MALL EAST AND COCKSPUR STREET, CHARING CROSS, LONDON, S.W.

ALL GOODS CARRIAGE PAID—SEE PREFACE.   EVERY ARTICLE IN CATALOGUE PHOTOGRAPHED FROM STOCK.

No. 202.
Oak, walnut, or mahogany
Chair, in morocco. £4.0.0.

No. 203.
Dark mahogany Old English
Writing Chair, in velvet or mo-
rocco. £6.15.0.

No. 204.
The " Bulwer" circular Chair,
with caned oval panels and
seat. £8.8.0.

No. 205.
Oak Chair, with carved leather
seat and back. £5.15.0.

No. 206.
Italian carved walnut Chair, in
velvet. 58s. 6d.

No. 207.
Italian carved walnut vis-a-vis Settee, in velvet.
£4.18.6.

No. 208.
Italian carved walnut Settee, in velvet.
£6.15.0.

No. 216.   *Carved Oak Pedestal Writing Table, with 11 drawers, carved frieze, panelled ends, top lined leather.*
4ft. 6in.   £8.10.0.

No. 217.   *Enclosed Washstand, with cistern, dressing glass, and fittings, with desk slope, complete.*   70s.

No. 218.   *Writing Table, with carved mouldings, of best manufacture, Hobbs' patent locks, top lined morocco.*   18 Guineas.

No. 219.   *Cabinet Pedestal Writing Table, cabinet part closed by folding the side cases and lifting the desk slope.   Desk and table top lined leather.*   17 Guineas.

No. 220.   *Enclosed Washstand with reservoir above, tip-up basin, and waste tank below.*   £7.7.0.

No. 221.   *Superior Spanish Mahogany Cylinder Enclosed Pedestal Writing Table, of best manufacture, good locks, top lined morocco.*
4ft. 6in.   18 Guineas.   *5ft.*   19 Guineas.

No. 228.
Superior two-tier Revolving Book-case, on plinth, best finish.
Oak, walnut, or mahogany, 70s.

No. 229
Wall Bookcase, with Cupboard in centre, 3ft.6in. by 3ft. high. In ash, 55s.
In oak, walnut, or mahogany, 65s.

No. 231.
Carved Oak Secretary Bookcase-Writing Table, two Cupboards, and five Drawers in lower part.
4ft.6in. £25.

No. 230.
Superior three-tier Revolving Book-case, on plinth, best finish. In oak, walnut, or mahogany. £6.15.0.

No 232.
Superior three-tier Revolving Bookcase, with panelled sides, in oak, walnut, or mahogany. £6.15.0.

HAMPTON & SONS,
PALL MALL EAST AND COCKSPUR STREET, CHARING CROSS, LONDON, S.W.

No. 238.
Antique solid carved oak
Cabinet Nest of 8 drawers,
secured by one lock.
£5.17.6.

No. 239. Antique solid carved oak Bookcase, upper part
(having adjustable shelves) enclosed with glazed doors,
lower part enclosed with 2 cupboards fitted with shelves, 2
drawers above. 3ft.3in. **8 Guineas.** *4ft.6in.* **12 Guineas.**
6ft.6in. **18 Guineas.**

No. 240. Antique solid carved oak
Corner Bookcase, upper part with
adjustable shelves & glazed door,
lower part, cupboard with shelves.
£5.15.0.

No. 246.
Carved oak octagon Table.
2 ft. 3 in.   £3.15.0.
2 ft. 9 in.   4.10.0.
3 ft. 3 in.   5.10.0.

No. 246ᴬ
Carved 20-in. Greyhound
Flap Table.   20s.

No. 246ᴮ
Carved oak 3-flap circu-
lar Table.   45s.

No. 245.
Antique richly carved oak Secretary-Bureau, with 5
drawers, with Secretary-fall enclosing pigeon holes
and 12 drawers, lower part enclosed with two deep
drawers, ends being panelled and carved.
20 Guineas.

No. 247.
22" × 32" Portfolio, on wal-
nut, mahogany, or oak stand.
48s. 6d.

No. 248.
Massive Jacobean finely carved oak Bookcase, with cupboard in centre
and drawer above, of best manufacture.   6 ft.   **17 Guineas.**

HAMPTON & SONS,
PALL MALL EAST and COCKSPUR STREET, CHARING CROSS, LONDON, S.W.
ALL GOODS CARRIAGE PAID—SEE PREFACE.   EVERY ARTICLE IN CATALOGUE PHOTOGRAPHED FROM STOCK.

No. 258.
Carved Chippendale mahogany Bookcase, with open underpart and carved plinth. 3ft.6in. 23 Guineas.

*No.259. Hampton's Patent Library Step-Easel, in finely carved oak. £7.15.0.
Ditto, plain oak, walnut, or mahogany, 90s*

No. 260. Richly carved Chippendale mahogany Bookcase, of best manufacture. 29 Guineas.

HAMPTON & SONS
PALL MALL EAST AND COCKSPUR STREET, CHARING CROSS, LONDON, S.W.

No. 263.
Oval mahogany Table, with 2 flaps
and a drawer. **60s.**

No. 264.
Massive carved oak antique Table, a reproduction of a very fine 16th
century table in the Musée Plantin at Antwerp. 5ft. × 3ft.3in. **7 Guineas.**

No. 265.
Solid oak square 4-flap Table, mak-
ing large square table when open. **70s.**

No. 266.
Carved oak heavy octagon flap
Table. 3ft. **58s.6d.**

No. 267.
Massive carved oak Table, very fine carving. *Best manufacture.*
Price according to size and finish.

No. 268. Oak, walnut, or mahogany octa-
gon Centre Table, on square columns, of
superior manufacture. 3ft.6in. **£7.15.0.**

No. 269ᴬ Billiard Marking Board, mahogany. 10s.6d.

No. 269. Improved Reversible-Dining and Billiard Table, the most simple and perfect combination. It can be interchanged in less than a minute by one person, there being nothing to remove. It is manufactured of the best materials, with slate bed, and indiarubber cushions.

7ft. × 4ft., making Billiard Table 6ft. × 3ft., mahogany, £24.
8ft. × 4ft.6in. ,, ,, ,, 7ft. × 3ft.6in. ,, £28.
9ft. × 5ft. ,, ,, ,, 8ft. × 4ft. ,, £35.

Each table includes 3 solid ivory billiard balls, 4 cues, rest, and marking board.

No. 270. Pool marking boards for 6 or 8 players, from 20s. Combined Billiard and Pool do. for 8 persons, as shown, 7 Gs.

No. 271ᴬ Mahogany Billiard Room Seats, with step platform. Covered in roan leather, 25s. to 30s. per ft. run. ,, ,, morocco, 30s. to 40s. ,,

No. 271. Full-size mahogany Billiard Table, on 8 solid 6-inch mahogany legs, slate-bed 1⅝-inch thick, fitted with patent improved low and fast cushions, table covered with best cloth. Price, including 12 cues, 2 butts, 2 rests, 3 full-sized ivory balls, marking board, brush, iron, cover, &c., complete, full size, 40 Guineas. 10ft. × 5ft. 35 Guineas. 9ft. × 4ft.6in., 30 Guineas.

No. 271ᴮ Circular revolving Cue Stand, with patent brass clips for 12 cues. 50s.

HAMPTON & SONS,
PALL MALL EAST AND COCKSPUR STREET, CHARING CROSS, LONDON, S.W.

No. 278.
Large Easy Chair in saddlebags, mounted on Utrecht velvet of good quality.
£4.15.0.

No. 279.
Spanish large Easy Chair, covered in rich deep pile Oriental rugs and fringes. £8.15.0.

No. 280. *Large Easy Chair, in fine antique Persian saddlebags, mounted on fine velvet, & trimmed with rich deep fringe & tassels.* £11.10.0.

No. 281. *Large Easy Chair, in very fine antique Persian saddlebags, mounted on fine velvet, upholstered in best manner.* £12.10.0.

Note. *This Chair is nearly as large as No. 283, but was taken to wrong scale by the Photographer.*

No. 282. *Mother Hubbard large Easy Chair, in saddlebags, mounted on fine velvet.* £10.10.0.

No. 283. *Very large Easy Chair, in rich antique Persian saddlebags, mounted on fine velvet & fringed, upholstered in best manner.* £13.10.0.

HAMPTON & SONS,
PALL MALL EAST AND COCKSPUR STREET, CHARING CROSS, LONDON, S.W.

No. 313.　Settee, stuffed all hair in best manner, covered in cretonne.　£7.15.0.

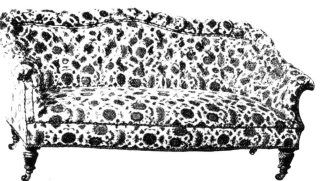

No. 314.　Settee, stuffed all hair in best manner, and covered in cretonne.　£8.10.0.

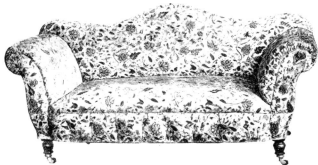

No. 315.　Prince of Wales Sofa, stuffed in best manner.　£7.15.0.

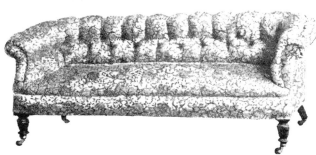

No. 316.　Chesterfield Settee, stuffed hair, and covered in cretonne.　£6.15.0.

No. 317.　Chesterfield Settee, stuffed and finished in best manner—very soft.　6ft.6in.　£8.5.0.　Larger sizes at proportionate prices.

No. 318. Vis-a-Vis, upholstered in best manner, with tufted border as shown. £7.10.0.
With plain edge 6. 6.0.

No. 319. Wall Settee, on square legs, stuffed hair, covered with cretonne. 5ft. £5.12.6. Other sizes, 23s.6d. per foot.

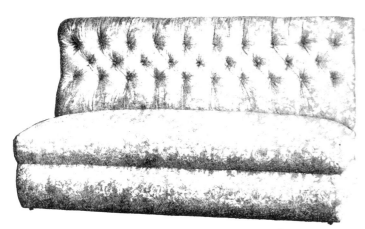

No. 320. Wall Ottoman, stuffed hair, covered in cretonne.
5 ft. £6.0.0. Other sizes, 24s. per foot.

No. 321. Six-Seat Centre Ottoman, stuffed hair, covered in cretonne. £14.14.0.
Flower pan and fringe, extra.

No. 324.

No. 324.

No. 325.

No. 326.

Louis XVI. and Adams Settees, Sofas, and Easy Chairs. A variety of old specimens and reproductions of the finest models of the various periods may always be seen in the show-rooms, covered in appropriate materials.

HAMPTON & SONS,

PALL MALL EAST AND COCKSPUR STREET, CHARING CROSS, LONDON, S.W.

ALL GOODS CARRIAGE PAID—SEE PREFACE.　　　EVERY ARTICLE IN CATALOGUE PHOTOGRAPHED FROM STOCK.

No. 336ᶜ

No. 336.

No. 336ᵛ

No. 337ᶜ

Mahogany inlaid Suite, consisting of Settee, 2 Arm Chairs as 336ᵛ, and 4 Small Chairs as 336ᶜ, covered in figured brocatelle. **24 Guineas.**

No. 337ᴬ

No. 337.

No. 337ᴮ

Rosewood inlaid Suite, stuffed all hair, covered in rich silk Genoa velvet, with plush borders, consisting of Settee, 2 Arm Chairs as 337ᴬ, 2 Gossip Chairs as 337ᴮ, and 4 Small Chairs as 337ᶜ **34 Guineas.**

HAMPTON & SONS,

PALL MALL EAST AND COCKSPUR STREET, CHARING CROSS, LONDON, S.W.

ALL GOODS CARRIAGE PAID—SEE PREFACE.   EVERY ARTICLE IN CATALOGUE PHOTOGRAPHED FROM STOCK.

No.355. Gossip Chair,
enamelled or bronzed
any color, covered in
silk tapestry. 14s.9d.

No. 356.
Gilt Occasional Chair.
14s. 6d.

No. 357.
Gilt Bamboo Occa-
sional Chair.
18s. 6d.

No. 358.
Mahogany inlaid Arm
Chair, covered in Genoa
silk velvet. 38s. 6d.

No. 389.
Mahogany inlaid and carved
Arm. Chair, covered in Genoa
silk velvet. 58s. 6d.

No. 360.
Queen Anne Chair, dark
mahogany or walnut.
58s. 6d.

No. 361.
Mahogany inlaid Arm Chair,
seat in Genoa silk velvet.
67s. 6d.

No. 362.
Mahogany carved Arm
Chair, seat covered in
Genoa silk velvet. 70s.

No. 363.
Mahogany inlaid Arm Chair,
seat covered in silk tapestry.
72s. 6d.

No. 364.
Mahogany inlaid Arm
Chair, seat covered in silk
Genoa velvet. 72s. 6d.

HAMPTON & SONS,
PALL MALL EAST AND COCKSPUR STREET, CHARING CROSS, LONDON, S.W.
ALL GOODS CARRIAGE PAID SEE PREFACE.   EVERY ARTICLE IN CATALOGUE PHOTOGRAPHED FROM STOCK.

No. 381. *Walnut or mahogany, with screw, covered in cretonne. 15s. to 25s.*

No. 382. *Dark mahogany, covered in tapestry. 35s.*

No. 383. *A variety of Louis XV. & other high-class music stools on show.*

No. 384. *Dark mahogany Music Ottoman, with box to hold music beneath seat. 33s. 6d.*

No. 385. *Dark mahogany Chippendale Music Ottoman, to hold music. 37s. 6d.*

No. 386. *Rosewood or mahogany inlaid seat, covered in silk. 52s. 6d.*

No. 387. *Rosewood or mahogany, inlaid seat, in silk. 55s.*

No. 389. *Mahogany inlaid revolving Music Chair, covered in silk. 70s.*

No. 390. *Rosewood inlaid Seat, covered in tapestry. 55s.*

No. 391. *Inlaid Ottoman Music Seat, covered in silk tapestry. 45s.*

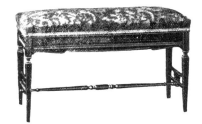

No. 392. *Duet Ottoman Seat, to hold music, in walnut or mahogany, covered in tapestry, 78s. 6d. Ditto, without box for music, 58s. 6d.*

No. 393. *Dark mahogany curved Duet or window seat, covered in brocatelle or tapestry. 90s.*

No. 394. *Inlaid rosewood or mahogany Duet Ottoman, covered in Genoa silk velvet or brocatelle. £5.15.0.*

No. 395.
*Walnut or mahogany,
carved, with shelf in
upper part, and five
bevelled silvered plates.*
£3.15.0.

No. 396.
*Dark mahogany Chippendale, with brass gallery,
door fitted with silk curtain.* **£4.15.0.**

No. 397.
*Rosewood or mahogany,
with shaped front & inlaid
panel.* **£5.15.0.**

No. 398.
*Rosewood or mahogany, inlaid
and carved moulding, with shelves
in back for china.* **£6.12.6.**

No. 399.
*Handsome dark mahogany,
carved Louis XV., best manufacture.* **£10.18.6.**

No. 421.
3 ft. 6 in. Richly carved mahogany China Cabinet, of best manufacture. **25 Guineas.**

No. 422.
4 ft. 6 in. Richly carved mahogany China Cabinet, of best manufacture. **24 Guineas.**

No. 423.
Louis XV. richly carved mahogany Cabinet, of best manufacture. **31 Guineas.**

HAMPTON & SONS,
PALL MALL EAST AND COCKSPUR STREET, CHARING CROSS, LONDON, S.W.
ALL GOODS CARRIAGE PAID—SEE PREFACE   EVERY ARTICLE IN CATALOGUE PHOTOGRAPHED FROM STOCK.

No. 440.
Mahogany dome top Chippendale richly carved Corner Cabinet, of best manufacture.
28 Guineas.

No. 441.
Old mahogany Pedestal.
42s.
Nubian decorated bust.
45s.

No. 442.
Louis XV. enamelled white carved Corner Cabinet, lined silk plush. 24 Guineas.

No. 443.
Old mahogany finely carved Pedestal. 7 Guineas.
Nubian decorated Bust.
45s.

No. 444.
Mahogany dome top Chippendale richly carved Corner Cabinet, of best manufacture. 33 Guineas.

No. 451.   *No.* 452.   *No.* 453.   *No.* 454.

No 455   *No.* 456.   *No.* 457.

These carved and gilt Chairs, together with many other reproductions of the finest models of the Louis XV. period, may be seen in our Show-rooms. The workmanship, in all cases, is of the best throughout. These, and all our Louis XV. and Louis XVI. Chairs and Settees, are also made in carved walnut and mahogany, dull polished, the details of the carving being enriched with gold, and in hard wood enamelled white, with carving gilt in same manner. Prices vary according to the treatment adopted and the covering selected. Quotations for any of the designs shown may be had on application, or special drawings, with quotations, will be supplied if desired.

HAMPTON & SONS,
PALL MALL EAST AND COCKSPUR STREET, CHARING CROSS, LONDON, S.W.

Specimen Cabinets in the French styles.　*Photographed from Stock*

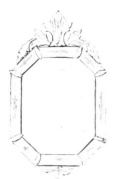

No. 502.
Venetian Glass Mirror.
45s.

No. 506.
Louis XV. Rosewood Inlaid
Show-case, with chased
mounts, lined silk plush.
9 Guineas.

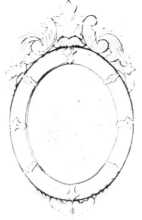

No. 503.
Venetian Glass Mirror, large
size.　8 Guineas.

No. 508.
Louis XV. Mahogany Cor-
ner Cabinet, mounted with
chased brass, marble top.
13 Guineas.

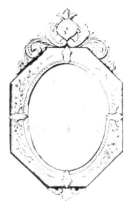

No. 504.
Venetian Glass Mirror,
large size.　90s.

No. 505.　Marqueterie
Nest of Drawers, with
brass mounts. 5 Guineas.

No. 507. Rosewood Inlaid Louis
XIV. Nest of Drawers, with chased
& gilt brass mounts.　8 Guineas.

No. 509.　Marqueterie Secre-
taire & Nest of Drawers, with
chased brass mounts. 9 Guineas.

No. 564.
Superior octagon Centre Table, in mahogany or walnut, 3ft. 3in. diameter. £4.10.0.

No. 565.
Superior circular Centre Table, in mahogany or walnut. 3ft. 3in. £4.10.0.

No. 566.
Superior mahogany or rosewood richly inlaid octagon Centre Table, with shelf under. 3ft. across top. £6.15.0.

No. 567.
Chippendale mahogany two-tier octagon Centre Table, on eight clustered columns.
2ft. 6in. £3.15.0. 3ft. £4.4.0.
Do., circular, on four clustered columns. 2ft. 6in. £2.15.0.
3ft. £3.0.0. 3ft. 3in. £3.10.0.

No. 568.
Chippendale mahogany octagon Two-Tier Centre Table, of superior manufacture. 3ft. across top. £5.15.0.

No. 569.
Louis XV. rich old mahogany Centre Table, very finely sculptured, of best manufacture and finish.

No. 595.
Chippendale mahogany 5-drawer Writing Table, supported on 8 clustered-column legs, with shelves below.
4ft.   9 Guineas.

No. 596.
Chippendale mahogany Cabinet Writing Table, of best manufacture and finish.
22 Guineas.

No. 597.
Chippendale mahogany Writing Table, fine model. Best manufacture and finish.
12 Guineas.

No. 598.
Pedestal Writing Table, shaped front, in mahogany, richly carved.   15 Guineas.

No. 599. *Louis XV. Writing Table, in rich Spanish mahogany, with shaped corners. Front & ends finely sculptured. Best manufacture & finish.* 21 Guineas.

No. 600. *Louis XV. shaped Pedestal Writing Table, in rich Spanish mahogany, elaborately & finely sculptured, best manufacture & finish.*
34 Guineas.

No. 601. *Mahogany inlaid Secretaire Writing Table, with tambour fall, lined complete.*
£8.10.0.

No. 602. *Rosewood inlaid Lady's Automatic Secretaire Writing Table, with tambour fall, fitted and lined plush.* **£9.15.0.**

No. 603. *Mahogany richly inlaid Cylinder Secretaire Writing Table, lined plush, of best manufacture and finish.* **13 Guineas.**

No. 604. *Walnut, mahogany, or enamelled white Screen Desk, with curtained book-shelves below, & shelves and velvet plaits for papers above. Folding tea cup shelf & music & paper rack at sides. Other side as 604ᴬ* **£11.18.6.**
A Screen Desk similar to above, but simpler in construction and finish, **£6.15.0.**

No. 605. *Mahogany inlaid large Davenport, cylinder fall and side drawers simultaneously locked by one action, best manufacture and finish.* **13 Guineas.**
The ordinary Davenport supplied, rosewood inlaid, from **65s.**

No. 604ᴬ *Reverse side of No. 604, showing cupboard with glazed door in centre between niches, hand-painted portraits in velvet frame above.*
£11.18.6.
Simpler finish, **£6.15.0.**

HAMPTON & SONS,
PALL MALL EAST AND COCKSPUR STEET, CHARING CROSS, LONDON, S.W.
ALL GOODS CARRIAGE PAID—SEE PREFACE. EVERY ARTICLE IN CATALOGUE PHOTOGRAPHED FROM STOCK.

No. 606.
Ebonized.
10s. 9d.

No. 607.
Ebonized.
11s. 9d.

No. 608. Carved Pedestal or Flower Stand.
27s. 6d.

No. 609. Carved Cupid Pedestal. £5.18.6.

No. 610. Large ebonized Pedestal, with Ionic capital. 28s. 6d.

No. 611. Rich mahogany or rosewood, mounted with ormolu, revolving onyx top. £4.18.6.

No. 612. Mahogany Adams, with inlaid medallion and satinwood bands. £5.10.0.

No. 613. Mahogany and other woods, mounted with ormolu. £6.6.0.

No. 614.
Louis XV. carved & gilt Pedestal.

No. 615. Adams Pedestal, in fine Spanish mahogany, richly inlaid on all sides.

No. 616. Louis XV. inlaid Marqueterie Nest of Drawers Secretaire Pedestal, with chased bronze gilt mounts and marble top. Choice selection in Showrooms.

No. 617. *Rosewood inlaid 2-fold Screen, striped silk panels.* 25s.

No. 618. *Enamelled white 2-fold Screen, with silk panels.* 45s.

No. 619. *Palm Stand or Wine Cooler, with brass bowl.* 52s. 6d.

No. 620. *Vernis Royal Cheval Screen, with embroidered panel.* £6.10.0. *In mahogany, with silk tapestry panel.* 78s. 6d.

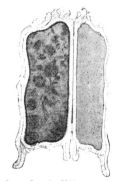

No. 621. *Louis XV. carved enamelled white 2-fold Screen, with silk tapestry panels.* £2.15.0.

No. 622. *Hand decorated Vernis Royal Adams pole-shield Screen.* 65s.

No. 623. *2-fold poker work Screen, with fluted silk panels.* 58s. 6d.

No. 624. *Mahogany Jardinere, with brass bowl.* £4.7.6.

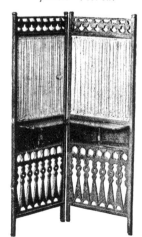

No. 625. *Tea Screen, with silk panel, and shelves.* £2.15.0.

No. 626. *2-fold Screen, with velvet panels plaited to hold photos, papers, etc.* 78s. 6d.

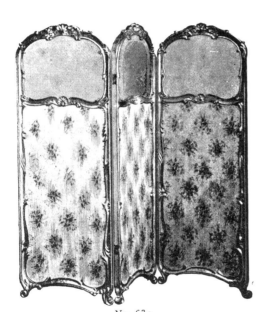

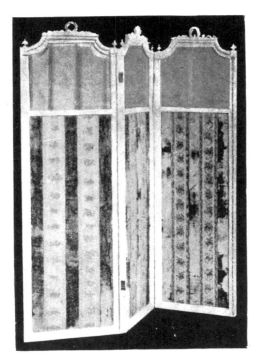

No. 630.
Louis XV. 3-fold Screen, enamelled white, panels
covered in tapestry   **17** *Guineas.*
     ,, best silk   **22** *Guineas.*

No. 631.
Enamelled white Louis XVI. 3-fold Screen, with
transparent bevelled glass panels at top, lower panels
covered in plush & striped tapestry.   **16** *Guineas.*

No. 632.
Richly carved graduated 3-fold Louis XV. Screen, top
panels bevelled glass, lower panels covered in silk
tapestry.   **15** *Guineas.*

HAMPTON & SONS,
PALL MALL EAST AND COCKSPUR STREET, CHARING CROSS, LONDON, S.W.
ALL GOODS CARRIAGE PAID SEE PREFACE.   EVERY ARTICLE IN CATALOGUE PHOTOGRAPHED FROM STOCK

No. 633 Enamelled white Mirror, bevelled silvered plate, bracket beneath glass. 19s. 6d.

No. 634. Dresden Mirror, with bevelled plate. 3 ft × 1 ft. 10 in. 12 Guineas.

No. 635. Rococo carved & gilt Mirror. 7 Guineas.

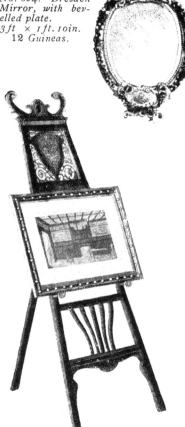

No. 636. Mahogany or walnut Easel. 55s.

No. 637. Fine mahogany richly inlaid Easel, best manufacture and finish. 6 Guineas.

No. 638. Enamelled white Rococo Easel. 4 Guineas. Gilt ditto, 6 Guineas.

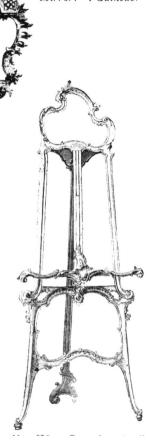

No. 639. Carved and gilt Louis XV. Easel. A choice selection of similar Easels in the show-rooms.

No. 646. *Mahogany or walnut.* 19s.6d. *Do., carved 36in. by 22in.* 44s.

No. 647. *Chippendale mahogany or walnut.* 39s.6d.

No. 648. *Chippendale, canopied, 34in. × 21in.* 75s.

No. 649. *Mahogany or walnut, carved, with 7 bevelled plates.* 42s.

No. 650. *Mahogany carved frame Mirror with sconces & flower holder.* £5.2.6.

No. 651. *Richly carved oak Mirror.* £5.15.0.

No. 652. *Chippendale Corner Wall Cabinet, in walnut.* 52s.6d.

No. 653. *White enamelled Hanging Cabinet.* £4.2.6.

No. 654. *Chippendale Corner Wall Cabinet, in walnut.* £4.15.0.

No. 655. *Mahogany inlaid Wall China Cabinet.* £6.18.6.

No. 656. *Mahogany Chippendale Wall Cabinet.* £4.10.0.

No. 657. *Mahogany carved and gilt Wall Mirror.* £5.18.6.

No. 667. *Mahogany & gold Mirror, with 3 bevelled plates.*
4 ft.7in. wide, 3 ft. high.   £7.18.6.

No. 668. *Enamelled white and gold Mirror, with 3*
bevelled plates 4 ft.9in. wide, 3 ft.6in. high. 8 Guineas.

No. 670.
Very handsome large Dresden Mirror, bevelled
plate. 4 ft. wide, 6 ft.6in. high. 45 Guineas.

No. 669. *Large Rococo Gilt*
Mirror, 5 ft. × 3 ft. 12 Guineas.

No. 671. *Carved Frame Chippendale Mirror, gilt*
in best manner. 5 ft.2in. wide, 5 ft.3in. high.
17 to 23 Guineas.

No. 692.
Mahogany Chippendale
3ft.11in. wide, 4ft.11in. high.　　7 Guineas.

No. 694.
Mahogany Chippendale.
4ft.9in. wide, 5ft. high.　£9.15.0

No. 693.
Mahogany inlaid.
5ft. wide, 3ft.9in. high.　　8 Guineas.

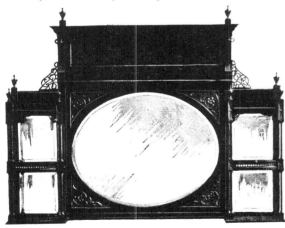

No. 695.
Mahogany Chippendale, carved.
5ft. wide, 4ft. high.　　11 Guineas.

No. 696.
Mahogany Louis XV., carved.
4ft.11in. wide, 4ft. 6in. high.　　£10.15 0.

No. 705.   Syrian inlaid
Koran Stand.
6in. wide, 21in. high,   7s.6d.
7   „   23   „   10s.6d.
9½   „   36   „.   25s.0d.

No. 706.   Arabian carved and inlaid Duet Seat,
covered in saddlebags and velvet.   £5.15.0.

No. 707.   Arabian carved inlaid
large octagon Coffee Table.
30in across.   £5.18.6.

No. 708.   Inlaid Syrian
Chair, with Mushara-
bêyeh panelling, seat
covered in rich mo-
quette.   £4.10.0.

No. 709.   Syrian in-
laid Ottoman Seat,
covered in saddlebag.
38s.6d.

No. 710ᴬ.   Arm Chair en
suite with Settee. £5.10.0.

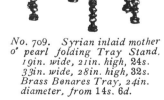

No. 709.   Syrian inlaid mother
o' pearl folding Tray Stand.
19in. wide, 21in. high, 24s.
33in. wide, 28in. high, 32s.
Brass Benares Tray, 24in.
diameter, from 14s. 6d.

No. 710.   Arabian Settee, carved, with Musha-
rabêyeh panelling, covered in rich moquette.
£9.15.0.

No. 710ᴮ   Chair en
suite.   75s.

*No. 717. Chinese carved black wood
Pedestal, with inlaid marble top. 22in.
across, 32in. high. 90s.
Handsome Bronze Jardineres from 30s.*

*No. 718. Handsome Japanese Cabinet, richly carved, & inlaid with carved
ivory & mother o'pearl, & enriched with lacquer decoration.　93 Guineas.*

*No. 719. Japanese Bronze Stork,
fine quality. 7ft. 6in. high.
£5.15.0.
Well adapted for holding electric light in beak.*

No. 748. Bamboo Hamlet Seat, covered in Japanese stamped leather. 18s.9d.

No. 749. Bamboo Chair with rush seat. 12s.9d.

No. 750. Bamboo Wall Bracket, 2ft. 4in. wide, 2ft.7in. high. 29s.6d.

No. 751. Indian carved Centre Table, 2ft.2in. across, 2ft.6½in. high. 65s.

No. 753. Richly carved shaped Corner Table. 2ft.8in. high. 90s.

No. 752. Hand-painted Screens, panels in assorted colors, with brocaded cloth backs and borders.

4ft. 6in. high, 8s.9d.	Superior Ditto, 15s.
5ft. 6in. high, 11s.9d.	Do. 17s.6d.

No. 754. Gold Embroidered Screen, brocaded borders, & cloth back. 4ft. 6in. high, 12s.6d. 5ft. 13s.6d. 5ft. 6in. 14s.6d. Superior qualities, from 17s.6d. to £25.

No. 761.
Bamboo & Matting Work Table,
lined with tufted satin. 32s. 6d.
Without sliding side shelves, 30s.

No. 762.
Bamboo Cabinet, with two cup-
boards with lacquer panels, and
bevelled glass in back. 47s. 6d.

No. 763.
Bamboo and lacquer Cabinet, with cupboards, and five
bevelled plates. 4ft. 9in. wide, 6ft. 10in. high.
11 Guineas.

No. 764.
Overmantel, with leather paper deco-
rated panels and bevelled plates.
3ft. 7in. wide, 4ft. 7in. high.
52s. 6d.

No. 765.
Bamboo and lacquer Writing Table, top
lined leather. 3ft. 3in. wide, 1ft. 11in.
deep. 70s.

HAMPTON & SONS,
PALL MALL EAST AND COCKSPUR STREET, CHARING CROSS, LONDON, S.W.
ALL GOODS CARRIAGE PAID—SEE PREFACE. EVERY ARTICLE IN CATALOGUE PHOTOGRAPHED FROM STOCK.

*No. 775. Bamboo Table, with
4 sliding flaps, octagon, round,
square, or oblong. 8s. 9d.
Square ,, ,, 2 flaps, 7s. 6d.*

*No. 776.
Corner 3-flap Table.
12s. 6d.*

*No. 777.
Lacquer top 4-flap round
Table, from 18s. 6d.*

*No. 778.
Lacquer top oblong 4-flap Table, from
18s. 6d.*

*No. 779.
Bamboo Canterbury,
with lacquer top and
panels. 13s. 6d.*

*No. 780.
Bamboo Music or Paper
Stand, with lacquer
panels. 13s. 6d.*

*No. 781.
Bamboo Pedestal.
9s. 6d.*

*No. 782. Bamboo Gong
Stand, from 8s. 6d. A large
selection of Gongs. from
5s. 6d. 10½ in. diameter.*

*No. 783.
Imari Umbrella holder
on bamboo stand.
32s. 6d.*

HAMPTON & SONS,
PALL MALL EAST AND COCKSPUR STREET, CHARING CROSS, LONDON, S.W.
ALL GOODS CARRIAGE PAID—SEE PREFACE.
EVERY ARTICLE IN CATALOGUE PHOTOGRAPHED FROM STOCK

No. 786. Consisting of Wardrobe, large Chest of Drawers, Dressing Table, Toilet Glass, Washstand with marble top and tiled back, Towel Horse, Pedestal Cupboard, and 2 cane-seat Chairs. £5.18.6.

No. 791. Consisting of large Wardrobe with bevelled glass, Dressing Table with shaped aud bevelled glass, Washstand with marble top and high tiled back, Pedestal cupboard, Towel-horse, and 3 cane-seat Chairs. Plain White, 20 Guineas. With hand painted floral decoration, 23 Guineas.

HAMPTON & SONS,
PALL MALL EAST AND **COCKSPUR STREET, CHARING CROSS, LONDON, S.W.**

ALL GOODS **CARRIAGE PAID**—SEE PREFACE. EVERY ARTICLE IN CATALOGUE **PHOTOGRAPHED** FROM STOCK.

No. 806. Butternut and burr-walnut Suite, of superior manufacture and finish, with carved panel, consisting of 4 ft. Wardrobe, with bevelled silvered glass panel to door; Dressing Chest, with jewel drawers and bevelled glass; Washstand, with colored marble top and high tiled back; Pedestal Cupboard; Towel Airer; and 2 cane-seat Chairs. **25 Guineas.**

HAMPTON & SONS,
PALL MALL EAST AND COCKSPUR STREET, CHARING CROSS, LONDON, S.W.
ALL GOODS CARRIAGE PAID—SEE PREFACE.   EVERY ARTICLE IN CATALOGUE PHOTOGRAPHED FROM STOCK.

No. 809.   Solid Ash Suite, consisting of 6ft. Wardrobe, with bevelled glass to centre door; Dressing Table, with jewel drawers and large bevelled glass; Washstand with marble top and tiled back; Pedestal Cupboard; Towel Horse; and 3 cane-seat Chairs.   £17.10.0.

HAMPTON & SONS,
PALL MALL EAST AND COCKSPUR STREET, CHARING CROSS, LONDON, S.W.
ALL GOODS CARRIAGE PAID—SEE PREFACE.   EVERY ARTICLE IN CATALOGUE PHOTOGRAPHED FROM STOCK

No. 816.   Superior Suite—consisting of 6 ft. Wardrobe, with 2 bevelled glass panels to doors of hanging cupboards, 6 drawers; projecting centre cupboard with moulded and carved panelling; 4 ft. Toilet Table, with jewel cupboards and large bevelled glass; 4 ft. Washstand, enclosed with cupboards and 2 deep drawers, coloured marble top, and marble tile back, with mirror; Pedestal Cupboard; Towel Horse; and 3 Chairs, upholstered in cretonne. In ash, 45 Guineas.   Mahogany or walnut, 49 Guineas.

HAMPTON & SONS,
PALL MALL EAST AND COCKSPUR STREET, CHARING CROSS, LONDON, S.W.

No. 847. *Ash, walnut, or mahogany. 17s.9d. Set of Ware for do. from 4s.11d.*

No. 848. *Ash, walnut, or mahogany, with marble shelf & top, cupboard & brass towel rails. 42s. Set of Ware, from 4s.11d.*

No. 849. *Oxford Washstand, with fittings, complete. 70s. Do., larger, with superior fittings & patent waste valve, 90s.*

No. 850. *The Cambridge Washstand, in ash, walnut, or mahogany, with earthenware top, tiled back, bevelled glass, & set of fittings, with towel rails, complete. £5.10.0.*

No. 851. *Enclosed Corner Washstand, with Rouge-Royal marble top and tiled back, of superior manufacture In ash, 75s. Walnut or mahogany, 78s.6d.*

No. 852. *Combination Washstand and Dressing Chest of 4 drawers and cupboard, marble top, tiled back and glass. In ash or walnut. 84s.*

No. 853. *Enclosed Corner Washstand, with earthenware lavatory top, of superior manufacture. In ash, 75s. In walnut or mahogany, 78s.6d.*

No. 868. *Strong linen Basket, Buff wicker & rush.* 4s.3d. 4s.9d. 5s.6d.

No. 869. *Corner Ditto.* 5s.6d. 7s. 8s.6d.

No. 870. 5s.9d. 7s.3d. 8s.3d.

No. 871. 4s.10d., 6s.9d., 8s.6d., 12s.6d.

No. 872. *Leg Rest, with double rising action, covered in leather.* 37s.6d. *Plain Do., covered in baize,* 7s.6d. *Bed Rests, with rising slope,* 25s. to 35s.

No. 873. *Patent Reading Easel, with Table Lamp & Leaf Holder, with ball lever action, to move in any direction.* 77s.6d.

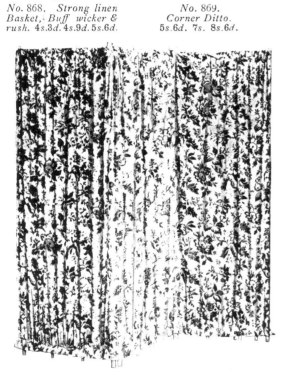

No. 874. *3-fold Rod Screen, for covering in cretonne or chintz. Polished pine,* 4ft. 6in. 20s., 5ft. 21s., 5ft. 6in. 22s.6d. *Enamelled white,* 4ft. 6in. 25s., 5ft. 27s.6d., 5ft. 6in. 29s.6d.

No. 875. *Dress Stand, in ash,* 35s. *Walnut or mahogany,* 38s.6d.

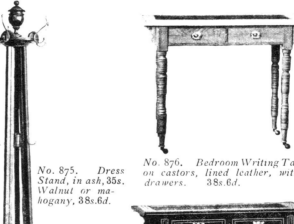

No. 876. *Bedroom Writing Table, on castors, lined leather, with 2 drawers.* 38s.6d.

No. 877. *Bedroom Writing Table, inlaid with 2 drawers.* 45s.

No. 878. *Invalid Rising Bed Table.* 45s.

HAMPTON & SONS,
PALL MALL EAST AND COCKSPUR STREET, CHARING CROSS, LONDON, S.W.
ALL GOODS CARRIAGE PAID—SEE PREFACE.   EVERY ARTICLE IN CATALOGUE PHOTOGRAPHED FROM STOCK.

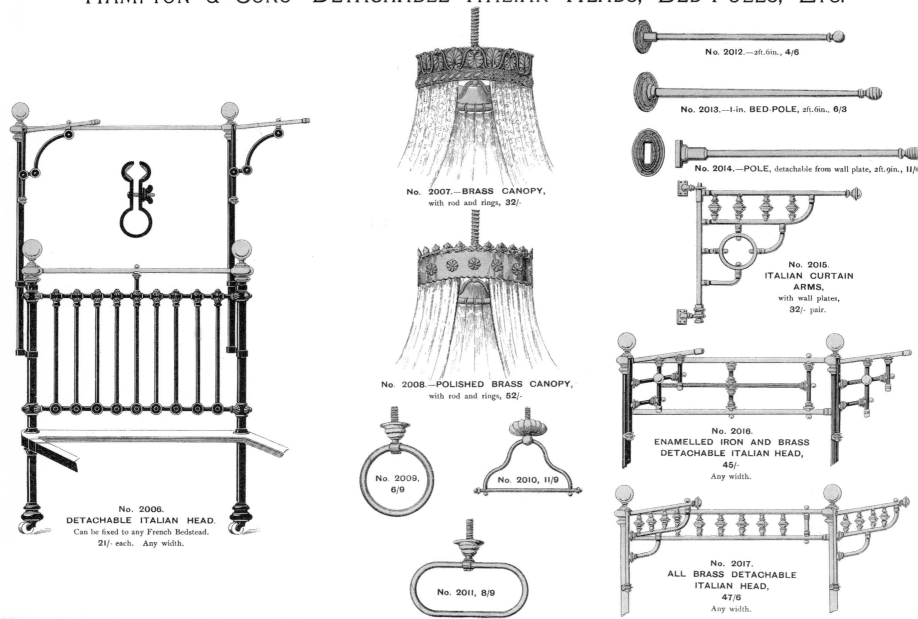

No. 2012.—2ft. 6in., 4/6

No. 2013.—1-in. BED-POLE, 2ft. 6in., 6/3

No. 2014.—POLE, detachable from wall plate, 2ft. 9in., 11/

No. 2007.—BRASS CANOPY,
with rod and rings, 32/-

**No. 2015.
ITALIAN CURTAIN
ARMS,**
with wall plates,
32/- pair.

No. 2008.—POLISHED BRASS CANOPY,
with rod and rings, 52/-

**No. 2009,
6/9**

No. 2010, 11/9

**No. 2016.
ENAMELLED IRON AND BRASS
DETACHABLE ITALIAN HEAD,
45/-**
Any width.

**No. 2006.
DETACHABLE ITALIAN HEAD.**
Can be fixed to any French Bedstead.
21/- each. Any width.

No. 2011, 8/9

**No. 2017.
ALL BRASS DETACHABLE
ITALIAN HEAD,
47/6**
Any width.

HAMPTON & SONS, PALL MALL EAST & COCKSPUR STREET, CHARING CROSS, LONDON, S.W.

HAMPTON & SONS' BASSINETTES AND COTS.

No. 2018.
FOLDING BASSINETTE,
japanned white or black.

2ft. 10 × 1ft. 7	3ft. 3 × 1ft. 7
24/6	27/6

No. 2021.
PATENT IMPROVED COT,
with sides to let down, woven wire spring mattress.

4ft. × 2ft.	4ft. 3 × 2ft. 3	4ft. 6 × 2ft. 6
28/6	31/6	34/6

No. 2020.
IRON AND BRASS FOUR-POST COT.

2ft. × 4ft.	2ft. 3 × 4ft. 3	2ft. 6 × 4ft. 6
71/6	75/-	78/-

ALL BRASS FOUR-POST COT.

94/-	97/6	100/-

No. 2019.
SWING BASSINETTE.

2ft. 10 × 1ft. 7
18/6

No. 2022.

2ft. × 4ft.	2ft. 3 × 4ft. 3	2ft. 6 × 4ft. 6
55/-	58/-	61/-

HAMPTON & SONS, PALL MALL EAST & COCKSPUR STREET, CHARING CROSS, LONDON, S.W.

HAMPTON & SONS' STUMP AND FRENCH BEDSTEADS.

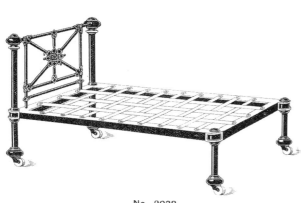

No. 2038.
VERY STRONG IRON STUMP BEDSTEAD.

2ft.6	3ft.	3ft.6	4ft.	4ft.6
9/6	10/6	11/6	12/6	13/6

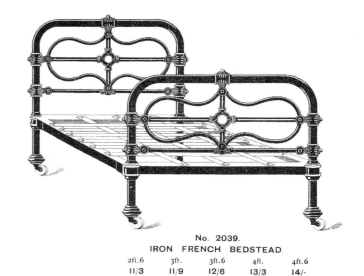

No. 2039.
IRON FRENCH BEDSTEAD.

2ft.6	3ft.	3ft.6	4ft.	4ft.6
11/3	11/9	12/6	13/3	14/-

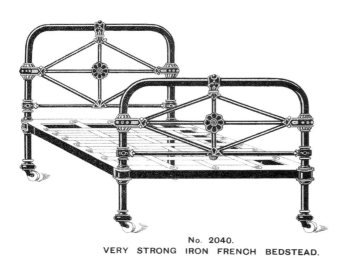

No. 2040.
VERY STRONG IRON FRENCH BEDSTEAD.

3ft.	3ft.6	4ft.	4ft.6
13/9	14/3	14/9	15/6

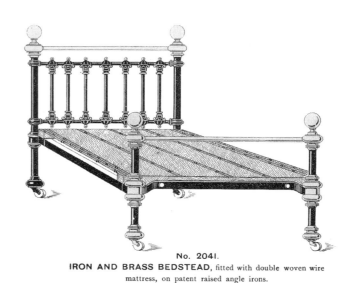

No. 2041.
IRON AND BRASS BEDSTEAD, fitted with double woven wire
mattress, on patent raised angle irons.

3ft.	3ft.6	4ft.	4ft.6
39/6	41/6	44/6	47/6

HAMPTON & SONS, PALL MALL EAST & COCKSPUR STREET, CHARING CROSS, LONDON, S.W.

Hampton & Sons' Black and Brass French Bedsteads.

These Designs Can Be Supplied As Italian or Half-Tester Bedsteads.

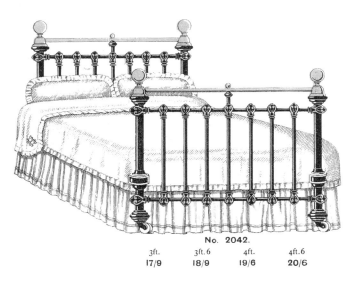

No. 2042.

3ft.	3ft. 6	4ft.	4ft. 6
17/9	18/9	19/6	20/6

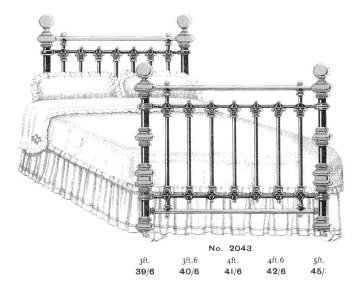

No. 2043.

3ft.	3ft. 6	4ft.	4ft. 6	5ft.
39/6	40/6	41/6	42/6	45/·

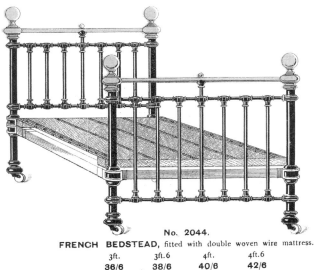

No. 2044.

FRENCH BEDSTEAD, fitted with double woven wire mattress.

3ft.	3ft. 6	4ft.	4ft. 6
36/6	38/6	40/6	42/6

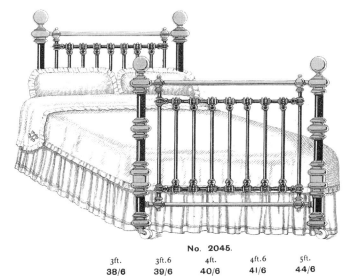

No. 2045.

3ft.	3ft. 6	4ft.	4ft. 6	5ft.
38/6	39/6	40/6	41/6	44/6

HAMPTON & SONS, PALL MALL EAST & COCKSPUR STREET, CHARING CROSS, LONDON, S.W.

Hampton & Sons' Enamelled Black and Brass Italian Bedsteads.

These designs can be supplied as French or Half-Tester Bedsteads.

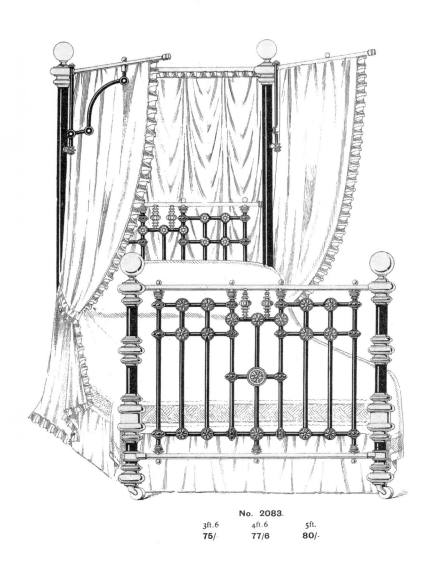

No. 2083.

3ft.6	4ft.6	5ft.
75/	77/6	80/-

No. 2084.

3ft.	3ft.6	4ft.	4ft.6	5ft.
£5 9 0	£5 11 0	£5 13 0	£5 15 0	£5 18 6

HAMPTON & SONS, PALL MALL EAST & COCKSPUR STREET, CHARING CROSS, LONDON. S.W.

No. 891.
*Ebonized, or stained
to represent any
wood.　4s.6d.*

No. 892.
Arm Chair.
10s.6d.

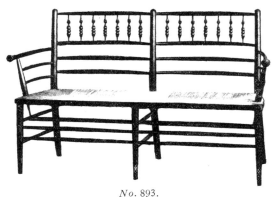

No. 893.

3ft. 6in. Settee	27s.6d.
4ft. ,,	32s.6d.
4ft.6in. ,,	36s.6d.
6ft. ,,	48s.6d.

No. 894.
*Ebonized, or stained
as any wood.　6s.9d.*

No. 895.
Arm Chair.　12s.6d.
Settee to match,
3ft.6in. 31s.6d.　4ft. 40s.
4ft.6in. 45s.　6ft. 60s.

No. 896.　*Ebonized, or
stained as any wood.*
11s.6d.　Arm Chair to
match.　16s.6d.

No. 897.　*Solid oak rush
seat Chair, quaintly carved,
well made, with under-
framing.*　16s.9d.

No. 898.
Arm Chair to match No. 897.
31s.6d.

No. 899.　*Solid oak rush
seat Chair, quaintly carved,
with underframing.*
24s.6d.

No. 900.
Arm Chair to match No. 899.
45s.

HAMPTON & SONS,
PALL MALL EAST AND COCKSPUR STEET, CHARING CROSS, LONDON, S.W.
ALL GOODS CARRIAGE PAID—SEE PREFACE.　　EVERY ARTICLE IN CATALOGUE PHOTOGRAPHED FROM STOCK.

No. 911. Birch, or stained walnut, or mahogany, superior quality, 13s.6d. *Without rocker,* 10s.9d.

No. 912. Ebonized, walnut, or mahogany. 18s.9d.

No. 913. Child's Table Chair. 14s.9d. to 25s.

No. 914. Walnut or mahogany Table Chair, of superior finish. 28s.6d.

No. 915. Chippendale mahogany, superior finish. 33s.6d.

No. 916. Folding Chair, with carpet seat and back 3s.9d. to 7s.9d.

No. 917. Folding automatic adjustable reclining Chair, stuffed in saddlebags and velvet. 42s.

No. 918. Derby folding Chair, without arms, polished birch, superior quality. 9s.6d.

No. 919. Derby folding Chair, with leg rest, in polished birch, superior quality. 20s. *Without leg rest,* 10s.6d. to 16s.6d.

No. 920.
Buff Wicker, covered and
draped in Madagascar
cloth. 10s.6d.

No. 921.
Buff Wicker, covered in
Madagascar cloth.
12s.6d.

No. 922.
Buff Wicker, covered in
Madagascar cloth.
13s.6d.

No. 923.
Buff Wicker, draped and
covered in cretonne.
16s.6d.

No. 924.
Buff Chair, draped & covered
in Oriental striped tapestry.
21s.

No. 925.
Buff Wicker Chair, covered in
Oriental striped tapestry.
25s.6d.

No. 926.
Large Buff Wicker Lounge Chair,
covered in cretonne, 25s. to 30s.
according to quality.

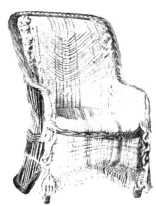

No. 927.
Large Buff shaped Seat Lounge
Wicker Chair, draped & covered
with Oriental metal-striped
tapestry. 32s.6d.

HAMPTON & SONS,
PALL MALL EAST AND COCKSPUR STREET, CHARING CROSS, LONDON, S.W.
ALL GOODS CARRIAGE PAID—SEE PREFACE. EVERY ARTICLE IN CATALOGUE PHOTOGRAPHED FROM STOCK.

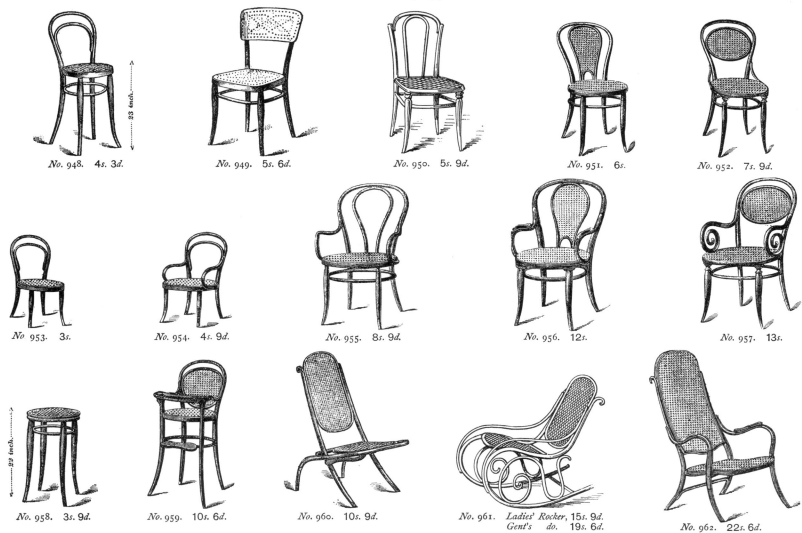

No. 948. 4s. 3d.

No. 949. 5s. 6d.

No. 950. 5s. 9d.

No. 951. 6s.

No. 952. 7s. 9d.

No 953. 3s.

No. 954. 4s. 9d.

No. 955. 8s. 9d.

No. 956. 12s.

No. 957. 13s.

No. 958. 3s. 9d.

No. 959. 10s. 6d.

No. 960. 10s. 9d.

No. 961. Ladies' Rocker, 15s. 9d.
Gent's do. 19s. 6d.

No. 962. 22s. 6d.

No. 963. Strong and cheap Chair. 2s. 6d.

*No. 964. Maple Veneer Seat, 3s. 10d.
Fibre Seat, ... 4s. 3d.*

*No. 965. Veneer Seat, 3s. 10d.
Fibre Seat, 4s. 3d.*

*No. 966. Veneer Seat, 4s. 9d.
Fibre Seat, 5s. 3d.*

*No. 967. Veneer Seat or Fibre
Seat, 5s. 6d.*

*No. 968. Oak Chair, Veneer
or Fibre Seat, 7s.*

*No. 969. Oak Chair, Fibre
Seat, 7s. 6d.*

*No. 970. Oak Revolving Chair,
Fibre Seat, 16s.*

*No. 971. Walnut or Oak, Fibre
Seat, 25s. Leather Seat and
Back, 38s. 6d.*

*No. 972. Fibre or Veneer Seat,
10s. 6d.*

HAMPTON & SONS,

PALL MALL EAST AND COCKSPUR STREET, CHARING CROSS, LONDON, S.W.

ALL GOODS CARRIAGE PAID—SEE PREFACE.   EVERY ARTICLE IN CATALOGUE PHOTOGRAPHED FROM STOCK.

No. 1.

A Portable Douro Chair, in Birch, Stuffed Hair, and covered in Leather, £2 17s. 6d.

No. 4.

Brass Hat and Coat Hooks, convertible into Stick Racks, 2s. 6d. each.

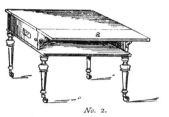

No. 2.

A Case to contain Chair, No. 1, arranged to form Table, £1 2s. 6d.

No. 5.

Brass Hat and Coat Hooks, convertible into Stick Racks, 2s. 6d. each.

No. 3.

An Iron Folding Cambridge Bed Chair, with Horsehair Cushions, in Best Leather Cloth, £4 12s. 6d. Case to form Table, £1 2s. 6d.

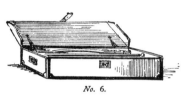

No. 6.

(See No. 7.)

No. 9.

No. 10.

No. 11.

Nos. 9, 10, and 11.—Mahogany Washstand, with Brass Standards, a Painted Oak Tub, the lid forming Table on Pillar and Claw Supports, Bottle, Glass, and Enamelled Fittings, £4.

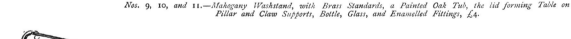

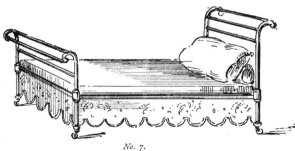

No. 7.

No. 7.—A Portable Iron Couch Bedstead, with Horsehair Mattress and Bolster, Feather Pillow, 3 Best White Blankets, a White Counterpane and Cretonne Cover and Valances complete.
No. 8.—A Black Waterproof Valise, to contain Bedding.
No. 6.—A Strong Iron-bound Chest, to contain Bedstead.

} *£11 complete.*

No. 8.

(See No. 7.)

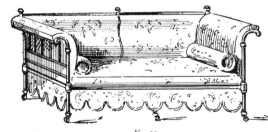

No. 12.

A Strong Portable Brass Sofa Bed, £7 18s. 6d.   A Strong Iron-bound Case for same, 11s.

HAMPTON & SONS,
PALL MALL EAST AND COCKSPUR STREET, CHARING CROSS, LONDON, S.W.

ALL GOODS **CARRIAGE PAID**—SEE PREFACE.   EVERY ARTICLE IN CATALOGUE **PHOTOGRAPHED** FROM STOCK.

No. 1000.

Fine Cast Mantel Register, with Ash Guard. Mantel painted any one colour. Price 21s. Size of Mantel, 24in. wide, 45in. high; Shelf, 27in. long, 6in. wide; Fire, 14in.

No. 1001.

Fine Cast Mantel Register, with Ash Guard and Tile Cheeks. Price £2.7s.6d. Size of Mantel, 36in. wide, 48in. high; Shelf, 42in. long, 6½in. wide; Fire, 14in. Mantel painted any one colour.

No. 1002.

Fine Cast Mantel Register, with Ash Guard and Tile Cheeks. Mantel painted any one colour. Price 50s. Size of Mantel, 37in. wide, 47in. high; Shelf, 43in. long, 7in. wide; Fire, 14in.

No. 1003.

Fine Cast Mantel Register. Mantel painted any one colour, fitted with Ash Guard and Tile Cheeks. Price £3.10.0. Size of Mantel, 42in. wide, 52in. high; Shelf, 48in. long, 9in. wide; Fire, 18in.

No. 1004.

Fine Cast Mantel Register, with Tile Cheeks. £2.10.0. Mantel painted any one colour. Size of Mantel, 36in. wide, 48in. high; Shelf, 44in. long, 7in. wide; Fire, 14in.

No. 1005.

Fine Cast Mantel Register, with Tile Cheeks, Ash Guard and Blower, 72s.6d. Mantel painted any one colour. Size of Mantel, 44in. wide, 51in. high; Shelf, 55in. long, 10in. wide; Fire, 16in.

HAMPTON & SONS,
PALL MALL EAST AND COCKSPUR STREET, CHARING CROSS, LONDON, S.W.

ALL GOODS CARRIAGE PAID—SEE PREFACE.   EVERY ARTICLE IN CATALOGUE PHOTOGRAPHED FROM STOCK.

No. 1014.
Fine finished Black Dog Grate, with brass mounts. Fire, 15in. Price £2.2.6.

No. 1015.
Fine finished Black Dog Grate, with brass mounts. Fire, 15in. Price £2.12.6.

No. 1016.
Wrought Iron Dog Grate, with adjustable Trivet & Brass Mounts. Fire, 15in. Price £3.8.0.

No. 1017.
Fine finished Black Dog Grate, with brass mounts. Fire, 17in. Price £4.5.0.

No. 1018.
Fine finished Black Dog Grate, with polished Brass Dogs and Mounts. Fire, 18in. Width of Dogs, 2ft. 8in. Price £6.0.0.

No. 1019.
Fine finished Black Dog Grate, with brass mounts. Fire, 18in. Extreme width, 2ft. 2in. Price £7.10.0.

No. 1020.
Fine finished Black and Brass Louis XV. Dog Grate. Fire, 17in. Extreme width of Dogs, 3ft. 3in. Price £9.0.0.

No. 1021.
Fine finished Black & Brass Adams' Dog Grate. Fire, 18in. Extreme width of Dogs, 2ft. 6in. Price £10.0.0.

No. 1022.
Fine finished Black and Brass Dog Grate. Fire 18in. Price £11.10.0.

No. 1042.
Solid Brass.
7s.6d.

No. 1043.
Brass Set, with
fluted Handle and
Knob. 8s.6d.

No. 1044.
Plain Heavy Brass
Set. 9s.6d.

No. 1045.
Brass Set.
12s.6d.

No. 1046.
Brass Set, Chased
Handles. 22s.6d.

No. 1047.
Copper and Brass
Set, Superior. 33s.6d.

No. 1048.
Brass Set, Lion
Head. 45s.

No. 1049.
Heavy Brass Set,
with Chased Head
and Bow. 52s.

No. 1050.
Superior Quality
Brass Set. 60s.

No. 1051.
Black and Brass Curb. Any size to 5ft. outside by 12in. inside. 32s.

No. 1053.
Black Curb, with Brass Rail and Supports, any size to 5ft. outside by 12in.
inside. 31s.0d. Ditto Ditto Polished Brass. 56s.

No. 1052.
Wrought Iron Curb, any size to 4ft. 9in. outside by 12in. inside. 48s.6d.

No. 1054.
Wrougt Iron Curb, with Copper Mounts. Any size to 4ft. 9in.
outside by 12in. inside. 57s.6d.

No. 1055.
Wrought Iron Curb, with Copper Scrolls and Corner Mounts, any size to 5ft.
outside by 12in. inside. 50s.

No. 1056.
Black Curb, with engraved Brass front and Brass-reeded Balls. Any size to
5ft. outside by 12in. inside. Price 40s.

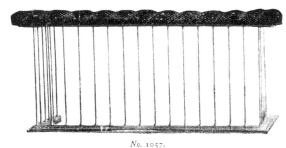

No. 1057.
Orleans Curb, with Seat upholstered in Morocco, Tapestry, or Velvets,
at prices from 75s.

No. 1058.
Fine finished Black Curb, with Reeded Brass Top Moulding and richly chased
Brass Ornaments on front. Any size to 5ft. outside by 12in. inside. £5.10.0.

No. 1059.
Set Fire Irons, on stand, all wrought iron. 22s.6d. Iron and Copper. 31s.

No. 1060.
Set Brasses, on polished brass stand. 26s. Larger set. 45s.

No. 1061.
Set Brasses on stand. 29s.6d.

No. 1062.
Set Fire Irons, on stand, all wrought iron. 30s. In copper and brass. 68s.6d.

No. 1063.
Set, complete, in copper and brass. 32s.

No. 1064.
Wrought iron and copper, complete. 45s.6d.

No. 1065.
Superior, all brass set, on stand. 48s.6d.

No. 1066.
Black and brass. 6s.6d. pair.

No. 1067.
Black and copper. 8s.9d. pair.

No. 1068.
Black and brass. 8s.9d. pair.

No. 1069.
Polished brass. 8s.9d. pair.

No. 1070.
Polished brass. Smaller size. 13s.6d. pr.

No. 1071.
Polished brass. 13s.9d. pair.

No. 1072.
Wrought iron, with brass vases. 14s.6d. pr.

No. 1073.
Wrought iron. 15s.6d. pair.

No. 1074.
Wrought iron. 24s.6d.

No. 1075.
Wrought iron, with copper mounts. 28s.6d. pair.

No. 1076.
Polished brass. 30s. pair.

No. 1077.
Black and brass. 30s. pair.

No. 1078.
Black and brass. 30s.6d. pair. All brass. 35s. pair.

No. 1079.
Black and brass. 32s. pair. Polished brass. 66s. pair.

No. 1080.
Copper and brass. 35s. pair.

No. 1081.
Polished brass, richly chased ball. 38s.6d. pair.

No. 1082.
Wrought iron, with bronze head. 50s. pair.

No. 1083.
Copper and brass. 52s.6d. pair.

No. 1084.
Polished brass. 63s. pair.

No. 1885.
Superior, large size, polished brass. 70s. pair.

No. 1086.
Brass trivet. 8s.9d.

No. 1087.
Brass trivet. 5s.9d.

No. 1088.
Brass plate stand, 8in. wide, 16in. long, 11s.9d. Larger sizes, 24in., 17s.; 30in., 20s.6d. 36in. long by 12in. wide. 22s.

No. 1089.
Brass folding plate stand. Size 20in., 14s.3d.; 24in., 16s.; 27in., 17s.6d.; 30in., 18s.6d.; 36in., 22s.

No. 1090.
Wrought iron and copper plate stand. 18in. long. 18s.6d.

No. 1091.
Wrought iron plate stand. 24in. long. 37s.6d.

No. 1092.
*Japanned, art colour. 3s.6d.
Brass or copper. 15s. Larger
sizes. 16s.3d., 18s.6d.*

No. 1093.
*Japanned black, brass mounts
and fitted lining. 6s., 7s.6d.,
8s.6d., 9s.5d.*

No. 1094.
*Japanned art colour, with
brass repoussé lid and mounts,
and inner lining. 15s.6d.*

No. 1095.
*15in. copper and brass, half
covered. 22s.6d.*

No. 1096.
*Copper Scuttle, with
wrought iron handle.
22s.6d.*

No. 1097.
*Copper Helmet Coal Scoop. 16in.,
29s.6d.; 17in., 32s.; 18in., 36s.;
19in., 37s.6d.; 20in., 43s. Brass
ditto, 16in., 35s.; 17in., 37s.6d.;
18in.,40s.; 19in.,43s.; 20in.,49s.*

No. 1098.
*Strong Copper Scuttle. 16in.,
30s., 17in., 31s.6d.; 18in.,
34s.6d. Brass. 32s., 33s.,
36s. Hand Scoop, 6s.9d.*

No. 1099.
*Copper, with brass mounts.
32s.*

No. 1100.
Copper or brass. 32s.

No. 1101.
*Copper or brass, with orna-
mented handle. 32s.6d.*

No. 1102.
*Wrought iron and copper
Log Basket. 32s.6d. Other
patterns always kept in stock.*

No. 1103.
*Polished brass, with em-
bossed lid, and fitted with
lining. 33s.*

No. 1104.
*Copper, with brass mounts
and fitted with lining. 35s.*

No. 1105.
*Polished brass or copper,
richly embossed lid and fitted
with lining. 37s.6d.*

iNo. 1106.
*Brass or copper, with repoussé
work on hood. 44s.*

No. 1107.
*Copper Coal Vase, with
wrought iron feet and galvanized lining. 57s.6d.*

No. 1108.
*Wrought iron frame, with
copper lining. 76s. Brass
frame, with copper lining.
84s.*

No. 1109.
*Copper and brass Coal Vase,
repoussé work on lid. 90s.*

HAMPTON & SONS,
PALL MALL EAST AND COCKSPUR STREET, CHARING CROSS, LONDON, S.W.
ALL GOODS CARRIAGE PAID SEE PREFACE.   EVERY ARTICLE IN CATALOGUE PHOTOGRAPHED FROM STOCK.

No. 1124.
14in. 16in. 18in. 20in. 22in. 24in.
Japanned wire, 10d. 1/ 1/3 1/6 1/9 2/
Brass wire, 2/2 2/10 3/4 4/6 5/3 6/
Strong „ beaded, 4/9 5/6 6/6 7/3 8/ 8/6

No. 1125.
Brass Stand Guard, 20in. wide, 24in. high, 7s.9d. Extra strong, 9s.6d. & 13s.

No. 1126.
Brass Folding Guard, 24in. wide, 18in. high, 14s.6d. Larger size, 16s.6d.

No. 1127.
Copper & Brass Folding Guard, 24in. wide, 24in. high. 17s.6d.

No. 1128.
Brass Stand Guard, with copper ornaments, 24in. wide, 26in. high. 22s.

No. 1129.
Brass and Copper Folding Screen, 28in. wide, 22in. high. 18s.6d.

No. 1130.
Copper and Brass Folding Guard, 28in. wide, 22in. high. 20s.

No. 1131.
Brass and Cathedral Glass Fire Screen, 22in. wide, 25in. high. 32s.

No. 1132.
Brass and Cathedral Glass Fire Screen, 21in. wide, 24in. high. 39s.

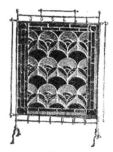

No. 1133.
Brass and Cathedral Glass Fire Screen, 24in. wide, 30in. high. 62s.

No. 1134.
Brass & Cathedral Glass Folding Screen. 65s.

No. 1135.
Brass Frame, with leaded bevelled plate glass centre, 20in. wide, 33in. high. From 82s.6d.

No. 1136.
Wrought Iron & Copper Stand Guard, with cathedral glass centre, 24in. wide, 33in. high. 92s.6d.

No. 1137.
Brass Louis XV. Stand Guard, gilt lacquered, 24in. wide, 33in. high. £7.18s.6d.

No. 1138.
A Louis XV. Rich Metal Stand Guard, finely chased, 28in. wide, 30in. high. £9.17s.6d.

No. 1139.
Polished Brass Kettle & Stand. 2-pint, 9s.6d. ; 3-pint, 11s.3d.;4-pt.,12s.3d.

No. 1140.
2-pint Copper Kettle, with wrought iron stand. 15s.6d.

No. 1141.
Copper Kettle, with wrought iron stand. 16s.6d.

No. 1142.
Brass Kettle & stand, 2-pint, 19s.6d.; 3-pt., 22s.; 4-pint, 24s.6d.

No. 1143.
Brass Kettle Repoussé and Stand, 3 pints. 21s.

No. 1144.
Repoussé Copper and Brass Kettle and Stand, 21s.

No. 1145.
3-pint Copper Kettle, with hammered top, on wrought iron stand. 21s.6d.

No. 1146.
Copper Kettle, with wrought iron stand. 22s.

No. 1147.
Handsome Brass Kettle and Stand, 45s.

No. 1148.
Wrought iron and copper, 19s.6d. Brass and copper, 32s.6d.

No. 1149.
Wrought iron and copper, 21s.

No. 1150.
Polished Brass Kettle and stand. 42s.

No. 1151.
Polished Brass Kettle and stand, 55s.

No. 1152.
Wrought iron & copper, 57s.6d. Polished brass & copper, 72s.6d.

No. 1153.
Wrought iron, copper, and brass. 68s.

No. 1154.
Polished Brass Stand, with walnut trays, and copper and brass Kettle. 72s.6d.

No. 1155.
Paper, Book, or Music Stand, brass frame, wood tray. 15s.8d.

No. 1156.
Music Stand, strong brass frame, with wood tray. 35s.

No. 1157.
Ornamental Music Stand, in wrought iron, copper, and brass. 47s.6d.

No. 1158.
Jardiniere, wrought iron stand, repoussé copper or brass pot, 30in. high, 8½in. diameter, 27s.6d. 34in. high, pot, 10in. diameter, 30s. Larger sizes to order.

No. 1159.
Jardiniere, polished brass stand, with richly embossed & frosted copper pot, 42in. high. £5.10.0.

No. 1160.
Jardiniere, wrought iron stand, very handsome design, copper pot, enriched with wrought iron floral wreath. 7.10.0

No. 1243.
Doulton Ware Vase, duplex burner, with plain globe, 14in. high to top of burner. 18s.

No. 1244.
Blue and White China Vase, duplex burner, plain globe, 13½in. high to top of burner. 21s.6d.

No. 1245.
Wrought iron and copper, with duplex burner and plain globe. 19in. high to top of burner. 24s

No. 1246.
Polished brass with duplex burner, plain globe, 17½in. to top of burner. 45s.

No. 1247
Copper and brass duplex burner, with opalescent globe, 16in. high to top of burner. 47s.6d.

No. 1248.
Reeded brass Column, with cut crystal head & duplex burner, plain globe, 24in. high to top of burner. 58s.

No. 1249.
Brass Lamp, duplex burner, and plain globe. 17½in high to top of burner. 63s.

No. 1250.
Handsome Brass Pedestal Lamp, duplex burner, and plain globe, 23in. high to top of burner. 70s.

No. 1251.
Polished brass, with cut crystal head and duplex burner, plain globe, 17in. high to top of burner. 82s.6d.

No. 1252.
Handsome brass Lamp for centre of dining table, with extending rod, and fitted with duplex burner and plain globe. Closed, 26in. to burner; extended, 36in. to burner. £5.7.6.

No. 1253.
China Vase Lamp, duplex burner and plain globe, 13½in. high to top of burner. 19s.6d.

No. 1254.
Brass Lamp, duplex burner & plain globe, 14in. high to top of burner, 22s.6d.

No. 1255.
China Vase Lamp, duplex burner and plain globe, 14in. high to top of burner 24s.

No. 1256.
Hungarian China Vase, duplex burner & plain globe, 14in. high to top of burner. 33s.

No. 1257.
China Vase Lamp, with duplex burner & plain globe, 15in. high to top of burner. 33s.

No. 1258.
Artistic brass and copper Lamp, duplex burner and plain globe, 16in. high to top of burner. 48s.

No. 1259.
Handsome repousse brass Vase Lamp, duplex burner & plain globe, 19½in. high to top of burner. 70s.

No. 1260.
Handsome brass Lamp, with extending rod; fitted with duplex burner, plain globe. Closed, 36in. to burner; extended, 44in. to burner. Suitable for central dining table Lamp. £6.0.0.

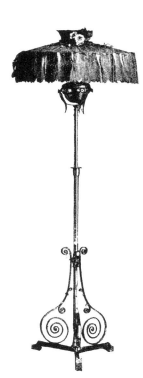

No. 1282.

Brass and copper Lamp, fitted with self-extinguishing duplex burner and chimney. 60s.

No. 1283.

Brass Lamp, fitted with self-extinguishing duplex burner and chimney. £4.5.0.

No. 1284.

Brass & copper Lamp, with automatic action for raising, and fitted with self-extinguishing duplex burner & chimney. £5.5.0. Wrought iron & copper. £4.7.6.

No. 1285.

Brass and copper Lamp, with automatic action for raising, and fitted with self-extinguishing duplex burner and chimney. £4.17.6.

No. 1286.

Brass and copper Lamp, patent action for raising, & fitted with self-extinguishing duplex burner and chimney. £5.10.0.

In all cases the Globes and Shades are an Extra.

HAMPTON & SONS,
PALL MALL EAST AND COCKSPUR STREET, CHARING CROSS, LONDON, S.W.
ALL GOODS CARRIAGE PAID—SEE PREFACE.   EVERY ARTICLE IN CATALOGUE PHOTOGRAPHED FROM STOCK.

No. 1297.
Wrought Iron Bracket. 9s.6d. Wrought Iron Lantern. 13s.6d.

No. 1298.
Wrought Iron Bracket. 20s. Wrought Iron Lantern. 21s.6d.

No. 1299.
Copper and brass Bracket Lamp, fitted with duplex burner. 23s.6d.

No. 1300.
Wrought iron and copper, fitted with duplex burner. 22s.6d.

No. 1301.
Wrought iron and copper, fitted with duplex burner. 33s.6d.

No. 1302.
Wrought iron Swing Bracket Lamp, fitted with duplex burner. 47s.6d.

No. 1303.
Richly embossed brass Bracket Lamp, fitted with duplex burner. 85s

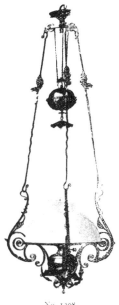

No. 1304.
Polished brass and copper, for oil, fitted duplex burner. £3.12.6.

No. 1305.
Wrought iron and copper Hanging Oil Lamp, fitted with duplex burner. 82s. 6d.

No. 1306.
Wrought iron & copper Hanging Shade Light, for oil, fitted with duplex burner & glass. £4.17.6.

No. 1307.
Wrought iron & copper Hanging Shade Light, for oil, with glass, complete. £5.18.6.

No. 1308.
Wrought iron and copper Shade Light, to draw up and down, fitted with duplex burner and glass, complete. £7.15.0.

No. 1309.
Lacquered or bronzed.
⅜ 8in. stiff - 1s.
½ ,, - 1s.4d.

No. 1310.
Polished brass, swing
bracket. 3s.

No. 1311.
Polished brass, double
swing. 5s.6d. Better
quality. 11s.6d.

No. 1312.
Polished brass, swing
bracket. 12s.9d.

No. 1313.
Polished brass, swing
bracket. 17s.6d.

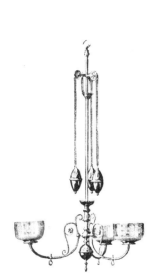

No. 1314.
Polished brass gaselier, with copper
relief. 2-light, 18s.6d.; 3-light,
24s.; 5-light, 40s.

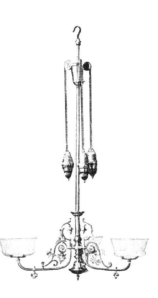

No. 1315.
Polished brass or bronzed. 2-light,
35s.; 3-light, 40s.; 5-light, 58s.6d.

No. 1316.
Polished brass and copper. 2-light,
29s.; 3-light, 37s.6d.; 5-light, 63s.

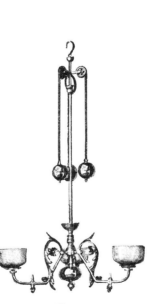

No. 1317.
Polished brass and copper gaselier,
£3.15.0.; 3-light, £7.0.0.; 4-light,
£4.8.6.; 5-light, £5.2.6.

No. 1318.
Handsome wrought and polished brass
gaselier, 3-light. £6.5.0.

HAMPTON & SONS' ELECTRIC LIGHT FITTINGS.

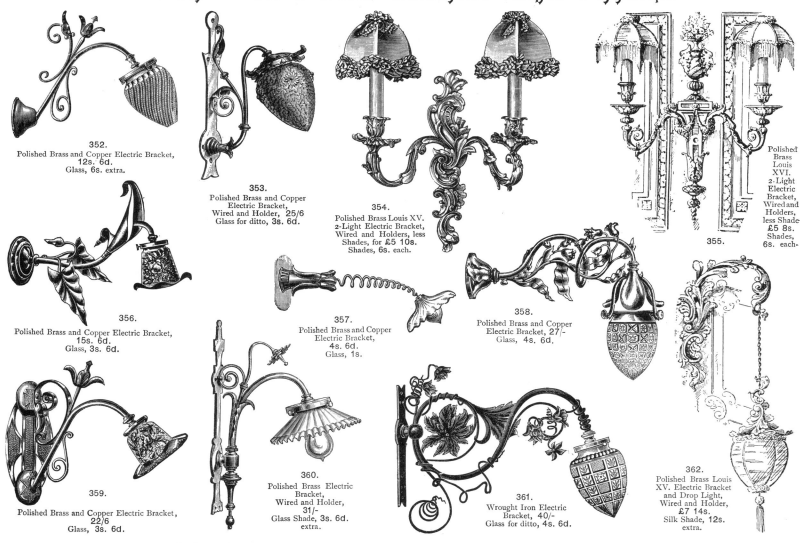

352.
Polished Brass and Copper Electric Bracket,
12s. 6d.
Glass, 6s. extra.

353.
Polished Brass and Copper
Electric Bracket,
Wired and Holder, 25/6
Glass for ditto, 3s. 6d.

354.
Polished Brass Louis XV.
2-Light Electric Bracket,
Wired and Holders, less
Shades, for £5 10s.
Shades, 6s. each.

355.
Polished Brass Louis XVI.
2-Light Electric Bracket,
Wired and Holders,
less Shade
£5 8s.
Shades,
6s. each.

356.
Polished Brass and Copper Electric Bracket,
15s. 6d.
Glass, 3s. 6d.

357.
Polished Brass and Copper
Electric Bracket,
4s. 6d.
Glass, 1s.

358.
Polished Brass and Copper
Electric Bracket, 27/-
Glass, 4s. 6d.

359.
Polished Brass and Copper Electric Bracket,
22/6
Glass, 3s. 6d.

360.
Polished Brass Electric
Bracket,
Wired and Holder,
31/-
Glass Shade, 3s. 6d.
extra.

361.
Wrought Iron Electric
Bracket, 40/-
Glass for ditto, 4s. 6d.

362.
Polished Brass Louis
XV. Electric Bracket
and Drop Light,
Wired and Holder,
£7 14s.
Silk Shade, 12s.
extra.

HAMPTON & SONS, PALL MALL EAST AND COCKSPUR STREET, LONDON, S.W.

ALL GOODS CARRIAGE PAID—SEE PREFACE.

Hampton & Sons' Electric Switches, Lamps, &c.

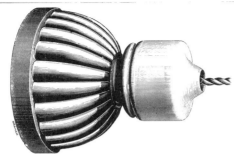

S54. Wall Plug, latest design for safety in use and convenience, as shown, with Brass Polished Cover ... 6s. 6d.

S 55. Ornamental Brass or Bronze Switch, 3 in. diam., as shown ... ... 7s. 6d.

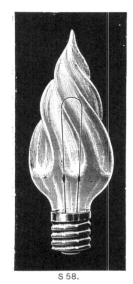

S 58.

Electric Lamps to represent the flame of a candle. Prices from 4s. 9d. each.

S 56.

"Elizabeth" Cream Porcelain Base with Polished Brass Cover, 2½ in. ... 3s.

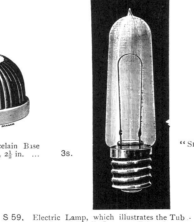

S 59. Electric Lamp, which illustrates the Tub-shaped Candle Lamps. Prices from ... 4s. 9d.

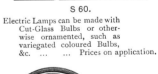

S 57.

"See-Saw" Switch, with Polished Brass Cover, as shown ... ... 4s. 6d.

S 60.

Electric Lamps can be made with Cut-Glass Bulbs or otherwise ornamented, such as variegated coloured Bulbs, &c. ... ... Prices on application.

S 61.

Ceiling Rose, with Cream Porcelain Ground, Gold Lines and Stars, 2½ in. ... ... 3s. 4d.

S 62.

"Key" Ceiling Rose, with Cream Porcelain Ground, rich Gold and Crimson Raised Decorations, 2½ in. diam. ... 3s. 4d.

S 63.

"Lincrusta" Ceiling Rose, with Cream Rough Porcelain Ground, with raised Decorations in Silver and Blue ... 4s. 6d.

S 64.

"Lincrusta" Cream Roughed Porcelain Ground, with Raised Decorations in Silver and Blue, 2½ in. ... ... 4s. 6d.

HAMPTON & SONS, PALL MALL EAST AND COCKSPUR STREET, LONDON, S.W.

ALL GOODS CARRIAGE PAID—SEE PREFACE.

No. 1379.	No. 1380.	No. 1381.	No. 1382.	No. 1383.	No. 1384.	No. 1385.	No. 1386.	No. 1387.	No. 1388.	No. 1389.	No. 1390.
Japanned, art colours, 7d.	*Japanned, art colours, 1s.*	*Japanned, art colours, 1s.8d.*	*Japanned, art colours, 1s.6d.*	*Japanned, art colours 1s.9d.*	*Japanned, art colours, 2s.3d.*	*Japanned, art colours, 2s.9d.*	*Japanned, art colours, 3s.*	*Japanned, art colours, 3s.*	*Japanned, art colours, 3s.*	*Japanned, art colours, 4s.*	*Japanned, art colours, 4s.6d.*

No. 1391.
Embossed copper or brass.
2-pt., 6s.9d.
3-pt., 7s.9d.

No. 1392.
Hot Water Can.
Japanned oak	2	3	4	6 pt.
	2/-	2/2	2/4	2/8
Polished brass	2	3	4	6 pt.
	5/6	6/-	6/9	8/9

No. 1393.
Toilet Can.
Japanned oak	4	6	8	10	12 qt.
	3/-	3/4	4/0	4/6	5/-
Polished brass	4	6	8	10	12 qt.
	10/-	11/9	12/9	14/-	16/-

No. 1394.
Japanned oak Foot Bath.
14	16	18	20	22 in
4/-	4/4	4/8	6/0	6/8

No. 1395.
Japanned oak Toilet Pail.
No. 1	2	3
4/-	4/8	6/-

No. 1396.
Japanned Sitz Bath.
No. 1	2	3	4
12/6	15/-	17/6	21/-

No. 1397.
Japanned Sponge Bath.
No. 0	1	1½	2	3	4
27	30	33	34½	38	44in.
12/6	14/-	15/-	17/-	19/9	25/-

No. 1398.
Japanned Oak Oxford Hip Bath.
No. 1	2	3	4
33	36	39	42in.
16/-	17/-	21/-	27/6

No. 1399.
Japanned oak Nursery Basin.
	20	21	23 in.
Round,	22/-	25/-	28/-
Oval,	24/-	30/-	35/-

No. 1400.
Oval Japanned Oak Travelling Bath.
18	20	22	24	28	32	36in.
11/-	13/-	15/-	16/-	18/6	22/-	25/-

Strong ditto, beaded edge.
22	24	28	32	36in.
21/-	25/-	30/-	34/-	38/6

  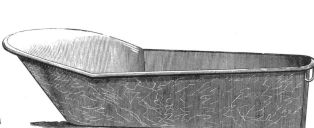 

No. 1401.
Japanned iron Washstand with china basin, 9s.6d.   Larger size with extra fittings, 13/3 & 25/-.

No. 1402.
Japanned oak Equal End Bath.
26	32	36	40	43	48	54	60	66 in.
11/6	15/-	16/6	20/-	27/6	31/-	42/-	48/-	59/6

No. 1403.
Japanned oak Taper Bath
51	58	62	66 in.
30/-	35/-	40/-	45/-

No. 1404.
Japanned iron Washstand with china basin and fittings complete. 28s.

HAMPTON & SONS,
PALL MALL EAST AND COCKSPUR STREET, TRAFALGAR SQUARE, LONDON, S.W.
ALL GOODS CARRIAGE PAID—SEE PREFACE. EVERY ARTICLE IN CATALOGUE PHOTOGRAPHED FROM STOCK.

No. 1405.
*Nursery Rocking Chair, stained mahogany
or birch, 7s.6d. Ditto, without rockers, 5s.*

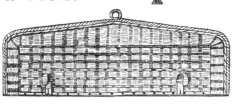

No. 1406.
*Washstand Screen, white, or white with red line, from 2s.9d.
to 7s.6d. each. Wicker Chair Backs, from 2s.3d. to 5s.6d.
Sponge Baskets, from 8d.*

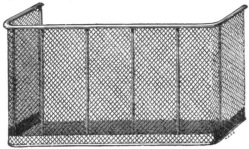

No. 1407.
Straight Wire Nursery Guard, Japanned any colour.

Width	2ft.6in.	2ft.9in.	3ft.	3ft.3in.	3ft.6in.	3ft.9in.	4ft.	4ft.3in.	4ft.6in
18in. high	10/9	11/7	12/4	13/1	13/10	14/8	16/2	17/8	18/10
24in. high	12/4	13/1	13/6	14/8	15/5	16/2	17/8	18/10	20/-
27in. high	13/6	14/8	15/5	16/2	16/11	18/6	19/8	20/9	21/6
30in. high	15/9	16/11	17/8	18/6	19/8	20/9	21/6	22/4	23/6

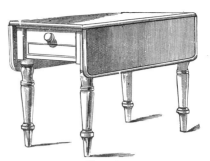

No. 1408.
*Pembroke Table, deal top, and stained mahogany
or walnut legs.   3ft., 15s.   3ft. 3in., 16s.9d.
3ft. 6in., 18s.6d.   4ft., 25s.*

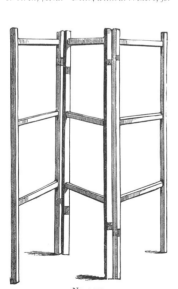

No. 1409.
*Deal Linen Horse.
2-fold, 4ft., 4s.   2-fold, 4ft.6in., 4s.6d.
3-fold, 5ft., 7s.6d.   3-fold, 6ft., 9s.6d.*

No. 1410.
*Nursery Table, legs and framing stained walnut or mahogany.
4ft.×2ft. 9in., 18s.9d.   4ft.6in.×3ft., 21s.9d.   5ft.×3ft., 24s.9d.*

No. 1411.
*Patent Duplex Step Ladder, with bar, in deal, stained & varnished.
5 steps, standing 3ft.6in. high, or ladder, 8ft. long (9 steps), 12s.6d.
6 "   "   4ft.6in. "   "   9ft.8in. " (11 steps), 15s.0d.
7 "   "   5ft.3in. "   "   11ft.4in. " (13 steps), 18s.0d.*

HAMPTON & SONS,
PALL MALL EAST AND COCKSPUR STREET, TRAFALGAR SQUARE, LONDON, S.W.

No. 1418.

Thuringian Porcelain Clock. 95s.

No. 1419.

Gilt bronze striking Clock, Watteau decoration. £8.10.0.

No. 1420.

Eight-day strike, Buhl and brass case. Height, 15½in. 95s.

No. 1421.

Brass Time-piece. 70s. Striking. 82s.6d.

No. 1422. **No. 1423.** **No. 1424.**

Dresden Clock, Four Children as the Seasons. Candelabra, 5-light, to correspond. Set of 3 pieces, £17.10.0.

No. 1425.

A choice selection of French Clocks of the best periods always kept in stock. From £7.15.0.

No. 1426.

Eight-day Timepiece, in oak or walnut case. Height 10½in. 17s.6d.

No. 1427.

A good selection of Japanese Clocks kept in stock.

No. 1428.

Eight-day ½-strike Clock, brass mounted dial, oak or walnut case. Height 16in. £5.18.6.

No. 1429.

Eight-day striking, oak or walnut case. 13in. high. 58s.6d.

No. 1430.

Quarter-strike, brass-mounted dial, oak or walnut case. Height 17in. 5 guineas.

No. 1431.

Eight-day Timepiece, in oak or walnut case. 38s.6d. Ditto, striking, Height 16in. 52s.6d.

No. 1432.

Eight-day ½-strike Clock, walnut case, brass mounted dial. Height 16in. 90s.

No. 1433.

English chiming Hall Clock in oak case chiming quarters and hours on gongs. 27 guineas. Ditto, chiming on eight bells and five gongs. 32 guineas. 23in. high, 14in. wide Bracket to match. 80s.

No. 1434.

Eight-day ½-strike Hall Clock, silvered and brass-mounted dial, oak case. Height 22½in. £6.18.6. Bracket to match, 30s.

No. 1435.

Best quality Aneroid Barometer, in polished oak frame and porcelain dial, with Thermometer, plate glass front. From 34s.6d.

No. 1436.

Gothic pattern Fitzroy Barometer, with Storm Glass and Thermometer, in best quality fumigated oak case, 31s.6d. Ditto, in stained case, 24s. Special designs for better cases sent on application.

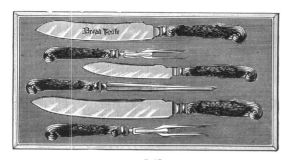

P 45.
Stag Horn Handles, Silver Caps and Ferrules, in Case.

3 Pieces, £1 10s. 6d.   4 Pieces, £2.   5 Pieces, £2 8s. 6d.   6 Pieces, £3 4s.

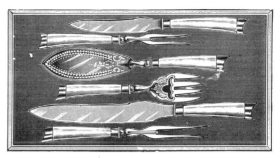

P 46.
Best Ivory Handles, Silver Caps and Ferrules, in Case.

3 Pieces, £2 16s.   4 Pieces, £3 7s.   5 Pieces, £4 6s.   6 Pieces, £6 12s. 6d.

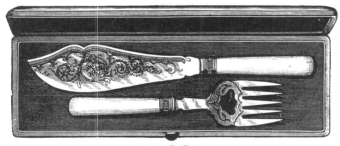

P 47.
Pair Ivory Handle Fish Carvers, in Case   ..   ..   18s. 6d.

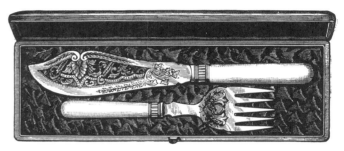

P 48.
Pair Ivory Handle Fish Carvers, in Case   ...   .   £1 1s. 6d.

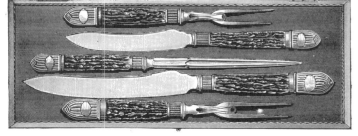

P 49.
Stag Horn Handles, with Silver Caps and Ferrules, in Case.

3 Pieces   ...   £1 10s.   4 Pieces   ...   £2.   5 Pieces   ...   £2 9s.

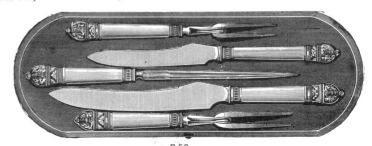

P 50.
Ivory Handles, Silver Caps and Ferrules, in Case.

3 Pieces   ...   £2 6s. 6d.   4 Pieces, £2 13s.   5 Pieces   ...   £3 3s.

P 51.

6 Spoons and Tongs ... £0 18s. 6d.
12 Spoons and Tongs ... 1 12s. 0d.
In Silk-lined Case.

P 52.

2 Spoons	£1	4s. 6d.
4 ,,	2	6s. 0d.
2 Spoons and Sifter	1	15s. 0d.
4 ,, ,, ...	2	18s. 6d.

In Silk-lined Case.

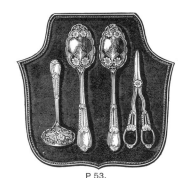

P 53.

4 Pieces, in Silk-lined Case ... ... £3 3s.

P 54.

Set, in Silk-lined Case, Richly Engraved 17s. 6d.

P 55.

Child's Plated Set, in
Case... ... ... 14s. 6d.

P 56.

Set 4 Salt Cellars and Spoons, in
Silk-lined Case, Best Electro-
plated ... ... £2 15s.

P 57.

Set 6 Napkin Rings, in
Case... ... ... 14s. 6d.

P 58.

2 Rings in Case, Plated
and Engraved ... 10s. 6d.

P 59.

Set 4 Salt Cellars, in Silk-lined
Case... ... ... £2 2s. 6d.

P 60.

Case of 6 Napkin Rings,
Best Electro-plate, and
Engraved ... ... £1 9s.

| P 15. FIDDLE. | P 16. OLD ENGLISH. | P 17. RAT TAIL. | P 18. BEAD. | P 19. ALBANY. | P 20. KING'S. |

CANTEENS.

SUITABLE FOR PRESENTATIONS.

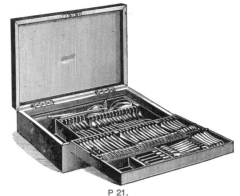

P 21.

Oak Box, containing :

	£	s.	d.
12 Table Forks ...	1	8	0
12 Dessert ,, ...	1	1	6
6 Table Spoons ...		15	0
12 Dessert ,, ...	1	1	6
12 Tea ,, ...		12	0
6 Egg ,, ...		5	3
4 Salt ,, ...		3	4
1 Mustard ,, ...		0	10
1 Soup Ladle ...		8	0
2 Sauce Ladles ...		4	8
1 Gravy Spoon ...		4	6
1 Pair Sugar Tongs ...		2	3
Oak Case	1	17	6
	£8	**4**	**4**

P 22.

Oak Box, flush handles, quadrant hinges, containing :

	£	s.	d.
12 Ivory Table Knives	1	6	6
12 ,, Dessert ,,	1	1	0
1 Pair Meat Carvers		9	0
1 ,, Game ,,		8	0
1 Steel		2	9
12 Table Forks ...	1	2	6
12 Dessert ,, ...		16	0
12 Table Spoons ...	1	4	0
12 Dessert ,, ...		16	0
12 Tea ,, ...		8	0
6 Egg ,, ...		3	3
2 Salt ,, ...		1	2
1 Mustard ,, ...		1	0
1 Soup Ladle ...		6	8
2 Sauce Ladles ...		4	0
1 Gravy Spoon ...		4	0
1 Pair Sugar Tongs ...		1	8
Case	2	16	0
	£11	**11**	**6**

					Rat Tail, Old English, and Fiddle.				Bead, King's, and Albany.	
Qualities					A1	I	C		A1	I
Table Forks, full size, per doz.	...	...	...	...	33/6	28/-	22/6	...	43/-	38/-
,, medium, ,,	...	...	...	...	30/-	25/-	20/-	...	—	—
,, small, ,,	...	...	...	...	27/-	23/-	18/6	...	40/-	34/-
Dessert Forks, full size, ,,	...	...	...	...	26/6	21/6	16/-	...	32/-	26/6
,, small, ,,	...	...	...	...	23/6	18/6	13/6	...	26/6	24/-
Table Spoons, full size, ,,	...	...	...	...	36/-	30/-	24/-	...	48/-	42/-
,, medium, ,,	...	...	...	...	32/-	26/6	20/-	...	44/6	38/-
,, small, ,,	...	...	...	...	28/-	24/-	17/6	...	—	—
Dessert Spoons, full size ,,	...	...	...	...	26/6	21/6	16/-	...	34/6	30/-
,, small, ,,	...	...	...	..	24/-	20/-	14/6	...	28/-	25/-
Tea Spoons, full size, ,,	...	...	...	...	16/-	12/-	8/-	...	22/-	18/6
,, medium, ,,	...	...	...	...	13/-	10/6	7/6	...	20/-	16/6
,, small, ,,	...	...	...	...	12/-	9/-	6/6	...	—	—
Egg Spoons, per doz.	...	...	...	...	12/-	10/6	6/6	...	20/-	16/6
Mustard and Salt Spoons, each	...	...	...	...	1/-	10d.	7d.	...	1/8	1/5
Sugar Tongs, each	...	...	...	...	2/8	2/3	1/8	...	3/8	3/3
Gravy Spoons, ,,	...	...	...	...	5/3	4/6	4/-	...	7/3	6/6
Soup Ladles, ,,	...	...	...	...	9/3	8/-	6/8	...	12/-	10/6
Sauce ,, ,,	...	...	...	...	2/8	2/4	2/-	...	4/-	3/3
Toddy ,, ,,	...	...	...	...	2/4	2/-	1/8	...	3/3	2/8
Fish Knives ,,	...	...	...	...	10/6	9/3	8/-	...	12/-	10/6
,, Forks ,,	...	...	...	...	8/-	6/6	5/3	...	8/-	7/-
Pickle or Oyster Forks, each	...	...	...	...	1/4	1/2	10d.	...	2/3	2/-
Butter Knives, ,,	...	...	...	...	2/8	2/4	1/10	...	3/6	3/3

HAMPTON & SONS, PALL MALL EAST AND COCKSPUR STREET, LONDON, S.W.

ALL GOODS CARRIAGE PAID—SEE PREFACE.

HAMPTON & SONS' CUTLERY AND ELECTRO-PLATE.

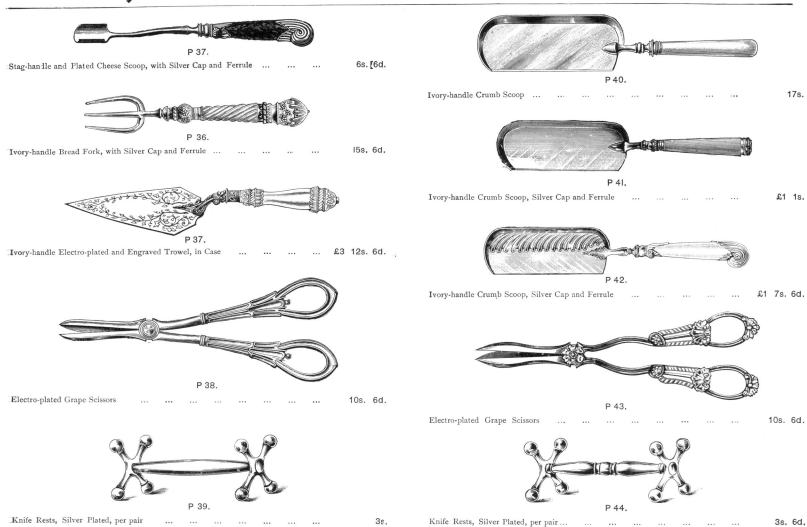

P 37.

Stag-handle and Plated Cheese Scoop, with Silver Cap and Ferrule ... ... 6s. 6d.

P 36.

Ivory-handle Bread Fork, with Silver Cap and Ferrule ... ... 15s. 6d.

P 37.

Ivory-handle Electro-plated and Engraved Trowel, in Case ... ... £3 12s. 6d.

P 38.

Electro-plated Grape Scissors ... ... 10s. 6d.

P 39.

Knife Rests, Silver Plated, per pair ... ... 3s.

P 40.

Ivory-handle Crumb Scoop ... ... 17s.

P 41.

Ivory-handle Crumb Scoop, Silver Cap and Ferrule ... ... £1 1s.

P 42.

Ivory-handle Crumb Scoop, Silver Cap and Ferrule ... ... £1 7s. 6d.

P 43.

Electro-plated Grape Scissors ... ... 10s. 6d.

P 44.

Knife Rests, Silver Plated, per pair ... ... 3s. 6d.

Hampton & Sons' Electro-Plate.

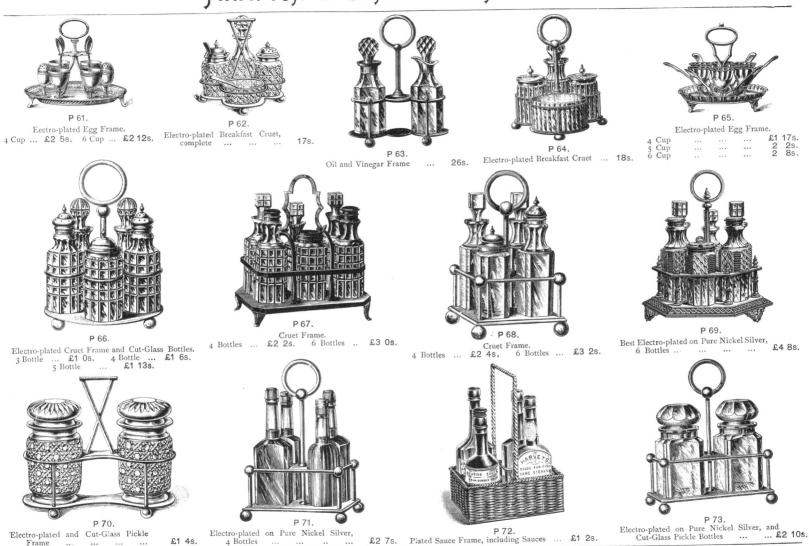

P 61.
Eectro-plated Egg Frame.
4 Cup ... £2 5s.   6 Cup ... £2 12s.

P 62.
Electro-plated Breakfast Cruet,
complete   ...   .   17s.

P 63.
Oil and Vinegar Frame   ...   26s.

P 64.
Electro-plated Breakfast Cruet ... 18s.

P 65.
Electro-plated Egg Frame.

4 Cup	...	...	...	£1 17s.
5 Cup	...	...	...	2 2s.
6 Cup	...	...	...	2 8s.

P 66.
Electro-plated Cruet Frame and Cut-Glass Bottles.
3 Bottle   ...   £1 0s.   4 Bottle   ...   £1 6s.
5 Bottle   ...   £1 13s.

P 67.
Cruet Frame.
4 Bottles   ...   £2 2s.   6 Bottles   ..   £3 0s.

P 68.
Cruet Frame.
4 Bottles   ...   £2 4s.   6 Bottles   ...   £3 2s.

P 69.
Best Electro-plated on Pure Nickel Silver,
6 Bottles   ..   ..   £4 8s.

P 70.
Electro-plated and Cut-Glass Pickle
Frame   ...   .   £1 4s.

P 71.
Electro-plated on Pure Nickel Silver,
4 Bottles   ...   .   £2 7s.

P 72.
Plated Sauce Frame, including Sauces   ...   £1 2s.

P 73.
Electro-plated on Pure Nickel Silver, and
Cut-Glass Pickle Bottles   ...   ...   £2 10s.

HAMPTON & SONS, PALL MALL EAST AND COCKSPUR STREET, LONDON, S.W.
ALL GOODS CARRIAGE PAID—SEE PREFACE.

HAMPTON & SONS' ELECTRO-PLATE.

P 74.

Set of 4 Entrée Dishes and Covers. 9 in. Dishes, £7 10s. set.
10 in. Dishes, £8 10s. set. 12 in. Dishes, £10 set.

P 75.

Set of 4 Richly Engraved 12 in. Dishes and Covers, £8 10s.

P 76.

Set of 4 Fluted Entrée Dishes and Covers, 12 in., £12 12s.

P 77.

Vegetable Dish and Cover, Best Electro-plated on Nickel Silver, with Ebony Handle, £4.

P 78.

£11 Plain, set of 4. If Fluted, £12 12s. set of 4.

P 79.

Vegetable Dish and Cover, Ivory Handle, £6 15s. Black Handle, £5 15s.

P 80.

Sauce Boats, Best Electro-plated. Small, 18s. Large, £1 5s.

P 81.

Sauce Boat, Best Electro-plated. Small, £1 13s. Large, £1 16s.

P 82.

Sauce Boat, Best Electro-plated. Small, £1 15s. Large, £2 2s..

P 83.

Best Electro-plated on Nickel Silver.

10 in.	12 in.	14 in.	16 in.	18 in.	20 in.
£1 11s. 6d.	£1 18s.	£2 4s. 6d.	£2 10s. 6d.	£2 17s.	£3 3s. 6d.

P 84.

Best Electro-plated Soup Tureen, 2 Quarts, £7 7s.

P 85.

Best Electro-plated on Nickel Silver.

10 in.	12 in.	14 in.	16 in.	18 in.	20 in.
£2 0s. 6d.	£2 9s.	£2 17s. 6d.	£3 5s. 6d.	£3 13s. 6d.	£4 1s. 6d.

HAMPTON & SONS, PALL MALL EAST AND COCKSPUR STREET, LONDON, S.W.

ALL GOODS CARRIAGE PAID—SEE PREFACE.

Hampton & Sons' Electro-Plate.

P 99.   14s.

P 100.   17s. 6d.

P 101.   £1 1s. 6d.

P 102.   £1 4s. 6d.

Tea and Coffee Set, Silver-plated on Best White Metal, £3 17s. 6d. the Set.

P 103.   £1 4s.

P 104.   £1 10s.

P 105.   £2.

P 106.   £2 6s.

Tea and Coffee Set, Silver-plated on Nickel Silver, and Richly Engraved, £7 Set.

P 107.

Tea Urn, A 1 Quality, Plated on Nickel Silver.

3 Pint ...   ...   £7 10s.
4 ,, ...   £8 12s.

P 108.

Kettle and Stand, A 1 Quality, Plated on Nickel Silver, and Richly Engraved.

2½ Pint £6

P 109.

Kettle and Stand, A 1 Quality, Plated on Nickel Silver, Handsomely Fluted.

2 Pint   ...   ...   £5 10s.

P 110.   £1 13s.

P 111.   £3 11s.

P 112.   £2 2s.

P 113.   £3 4s.

Queen Anne Tea and Coffee Set, Handsomely Fluted and Silver-plated on Nickel Silver, £10 10s. Set.

P 114.   £2.

P 115.   £4.

P 116.   £2 12s. 6d.

P 117.   £3 12s. 6d.

Tea and Coffee Set, Plated on Nickel Silver, and Richly Engraved, £12 5s. Set.

FOR PARTICULARS AND SCALE OF PRICES SEE OPPOSITE PAGE.

FOR PARTICULARS AND SCALE OF PRICES SEE OPPOSITE PAGE.

A.   B.   C.   D.   E.   F.   G.

H.   I.   J.   K.   L.

M.   N.   O.   P.

Please Note that Crested Services require about Six Weeks to Manufacture, except an Initial Service, which can be had in Three Weeks.

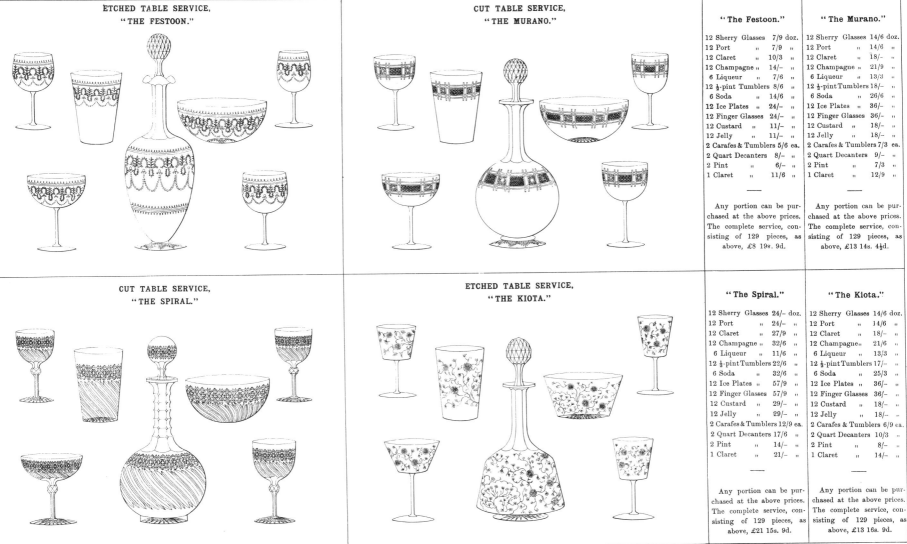

ETCHED TABLE SERVICE,
"THE FESTOON."

CUT TABLE SERVICE,
"THE MURANO."

CUT TABLE SERVICE,
"THE SPIRAL."

ETCHED TABLE SERVICE,
"THE KIOTA."

"The Festoon."

12 Sherry Glasses	7/9	doz.
12 Port	7/9	„
12 Claret	10/3	„
12 Champagne	14/–	„
6 Liqueur	7/6	„
12 ½-pint Tumblers	8/6	„
6 Soda	14/6	„
12 Ice Plates	24/–	„
12 Finger Glasses	24/–	„
12 Custard	11/–	„
12 Jelly	11/–	„
2 Carafes & Tumblers	5/6	ea.
2 Quart Decanters	8/–	„
2 Pint	6/–	„
1 Claret	11/6	

Any portion can be purchased at the above prices. The complete service, consisting of 129 pieces, as above, £8 19s. 9d.

"The Murano."

12 Sherry Glasses	14/6	doz.
12 Port	14/6	„
12 Claret	18/–	„
12 Champagne	21/9	„
6 Liqueur	13/3	„
12 ½-pint Tumblers	18/–	„
6 Soda	26/6	„
12 Ice Plates	36/–	„
12 Finger Glasses	36/–	„
12 Custard	18/–	„
12 Jelly	18/–	„
2 Carafes & Tumblers	7/3	ea.
2 Quart Decanters	9/–	„
2 Pint	7/3	„
1 Claret	12/9	

Any portion can be purchased at the above prices. The complete service, consisting of 129 pieces, as above, £13 14s. 4½d.

"The Spiral."

12 Sherry Glasses	24/–	doz.
12 Port	24/–	„
12 Claret	27/9	„
12 Champagne	32/6	„
6 Liqueur	11/6	„
12 ½-pint Tumblers	22/6	„
6 Soda	32/6	„
12 Ice Plates	57/9	„
12 Finger Glasses	57/9	„
12 Custard	29/–	„
12 Jelly	29/–	„
2 Carafes & Tumblers	12/9	ea.
2 Quart Decanters	17/6	„
2 Pint	14/–	„
1 Claret	21/–	„

Any portion can be purchased at the above prices. The complete service, consisting of 129 pieces, as above, £21 15s. 9d.

"The Kiota."

12 Sherry Glasses	14/6	doz.
12 Port	14/6	„
12 Claret	18/–	„
12 Champagne	21/6	„
6 Liqueur	13/3	„
12 ½-pint Tumblers	17/–	„
6 Soda	25/3	„
12 Ice Plates	36/–	„
12 Finger Glasses	36/–	„
12 Custard	18/–	„
12 Jelly	18/–	„
2 Carafes & Tumblers	6/9	ea.
2 Quart Decanters	10/3	„
2 Pint	8/–	„
1 Claret	14/–	„

Any portion can be purchased at the above prices. The complete service, consisting of 129 pieces, as above, £13 16s. 9d.

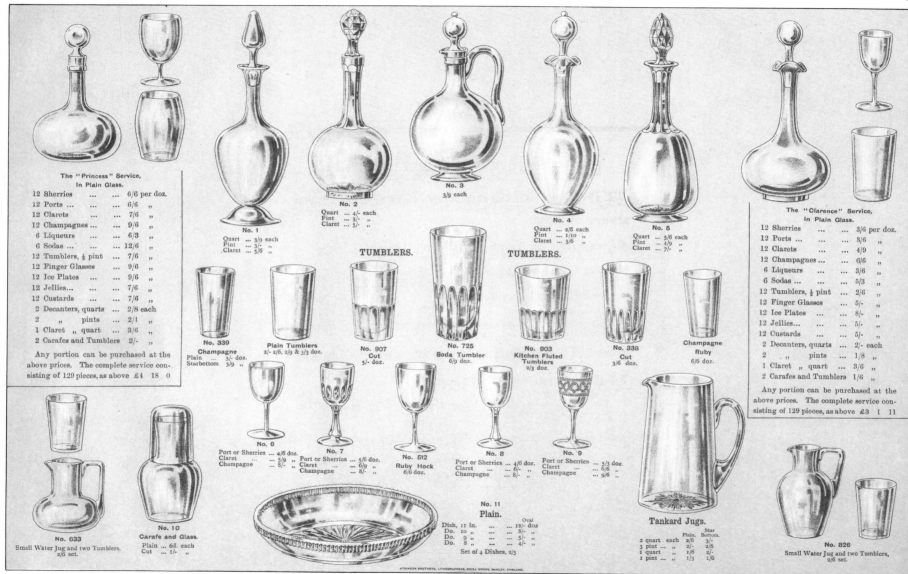

The "Princess" Service,
In Plain Glass.

12 Sherries	...	...	6/6 per doz.
12 Ports	...	...	6/6 ,,
12 Clarets	...	...	7/6 ,,
12 Champagnes	...	...	9/6 ,,
6 Liqueurs	...	...	6/3 ,,
6 Sodas	...	...	12/6 ,,
12 Tumblers, ½ pint	...	7/6 ,,
12 Finger Glasses	...	9/6 ,,
12 Ice Plates	...	...	9/6 ,,
12 Jellies	...	...	7/6 ,,
12 Custards	...	...	7/6 ,,
2 Decanters, quarts	...	2/8 each
2 ,, pints	...	2/1 ,,
1 Claret ,, quart	...	3/6 ,,
2 Carafes and Tumblers	2/- ,,

Any portion can be purchased at the above prices. The complete service consisting of 129 pieces, as above £4 18 0

No. 1
Quart ... 3/9 each
Pint ... 3/- ,,
Claret ... 5/6 ,,

No. 2
Quart ... 4/- each
Pint ... 3/- ,,
Claret ... 5/- ,,

No. 3
3/9 each

No. 4
Quart ... 2/6 each
Pint ... 1/10 ,,
Claret ... 3/6 ,,

No. 5
Quart ... 5/6 each
Pint ... 4/9 ,,
Claret ... 7/- ,,

The "Clarence" Service,
In Plain Glass.

12 Sherries	...	...	3/6 per doz.
12 Ports	...	...	3/6 ,,
12 Clarets	...	...	4/9 ,,
12 Champagnes	...	6/6 ,,
6 Liqueurs	...	...	3/6 ,,
6 Sodas	...	...	5/3 ,,
12 Tumblers, ½ pint	...	2/6 ,,
12 Finger Glasses	...	5/- ,,
12 Ice Plates	...	...	8/- ,,
12 Jellies	...	...	5/- ,,
12 Custards	...	...	5/- ,,
2 Decanters, quarts	...	2/- each
2 ,, pints	...	1/8 ,,
1 Claret ,, quart	...	3/6 ,,
2 Carafes and Tumblers	1/6 ,,

Any portion can be purchased at the above prices. The complete service consisting of 129 pieces, as above £3 1 11

TUMBLERS.

TUMBLERS.

No. 339
Champagne
Plain ... 3/- doz.
Starbottom 3/9 ,,

Plain Tumblers
2/- 2/6, 2/9 & 3/3 doz.

No. 907
Cut
5/- doz.

No. 725
Soda Tumbler
6/9 doz.

No. 903
Kitchen Fluted
Tumblers
2/3 doz.

No. 338
Cut
3/6 doz.

Champagne
Ruby
6/6 doz.

No. 6
Port or Sherries ... 4/6 doz.
Claret ... 5/9 ,,
Champagne ... 8/- ,,

No. 7
Port or Sherries ... 5/6 doz.
Claret ... 6/9 ,,
Champagne ... 8/- ,,

No. 512
Ruby Hock
6/6 doz.

No. 8
Port or Sherries ... 4/6 doz.
Claret ... 6/- ,,
Champagne ... 8/- ,,

No. 9
Port or Sherries ... 5/3 doz.
Claret ... 6/6 ,,
Champagne ... 9/6 ,,

No. 633
Small Water Jug and two Tumblers,
2/6 set.

No. 10
Carafe and Glass.
Plain ... 6d. each
Cut ... 1/- ,,

No. 11
Plain.

				Oval
Dish, 11 in.	...	...	...	12/- doz
Do. 10 ,,	...	...	...	8/- ,,
Do. 9 ,,	...	...	...	5/- ,,
Do. 8 ,,	...	...	...	4/- ,,
Set of 4 Dishes, 2/5				

Tankard Jugs.

	Plain.	Star Bottom.
2 quart each	2/6	3/-
3 pint ,,	2/3	2/6
1 quart ,,	1/6	2/-
1 pint ,,	1/3	1/6

No. 826
Small Water Jug and two Tumblers,
2/6 set.

HAMPTON & SONS, PALL MALL EAST & COCKSPUR STREET, CHARING CROSS, LONDON, S.W.

Coffee Pot, Long Spout
(Brown)

¾ pint ... 10d. each.
1 ,, ... 1/2 ,,

Oval Eared Dish
(White)

diam.
6 in. ... 5d. each
7 ,, ... 5½d. ,,
8 ,, ... 6½d. ,,
9 ,, ... 8d. ,,
10 ,, ... 10d. ,,
11 ,, ... 1/3 ,,

Coffee Pot & Filter
(Brown)

1 cup ... 1/3 each
2 ,, ... 1/4 ,,
3 ,, ... 1/8 ,,
4 ,, ... 2/- ,,
5 ,, ... 2/6 ,,
6 ,, ... 3/- ,,

Oval Covered Pie Dish
(Brown)

9 in. ... 3/- each.
8½ ,, ... 2/6 ,,
8 ,, ... 2/2 ,,
7½ ,, ... 1/10 ,,

Milk Boilers
(Brown)

1½ pint 2/2 each
1 ,, ... 2/- ,,
½ ,, ... 1/5 ,,

Saucepan
(Brown)

½ pint ... 1/- each
¾ ,, ... 1/2 ,,
1 ,, ... 1/3 ,,
1½ ,, ... 1/6 ,,
1½ ,, ... 2/- ,,
2½ ,, ... 2/2 ,,

Tea Pot, London
(Brown)

2½ pint ... 2/6 each.
2 ,, ... 2/- ,,
1½ ,, ... 1/6 ,,
1 ,, ... 1/4 ,,
¾ ,, ... 1/2 ,,

The above are all Fireproof China.

Pudding Bowls

diam.
About 12 in ... 1/9 each.
,, 11 ,, ... 1/4 ,,
,, 10 ,, ... 10d. ,,
,, 9½ ,, ... 6½d. ,,
,, 8½ ,, ... 4½d. ,,
,, 7½ ,, ... 3d. ,,
,, 7 ,, ... 2d. ,,
Set of 7, 5/3 (one of each size).

Tea Pots
Rockingham (best). Mess Shape

To hold about ⅓ pint ... 6d. each.
,, ,, ½ ,, ... 8d. ,,
,, ,, ¾ ,, ... 9d. ,,
,, ,, 1¼ ,, ... 1/- ,,
,, ,, 1½ ,, ... 1/4 ,,

Kitchen Pans
(White, marked with letter K)

7 in. ... 7d. 12 in. ... 1/5
8 ,, ... 8d. 13 ,, ... 1/8
9 ,, ... 9d. 14 ,, ... 2/3
10 ,, ... 1/- 15 ,, ... 2/10
11 ,, ... 1/1 16 ,, ... 3/6

Plain Rockingham Tea Pots
(Best)

To hold 2 cups ... 5d. each.
,, 3 ,, ... 5d. ,,
,, 4 ,, ... 6d. ,,
,, 6 ,, ... 8d. ,,
,, 8 ,, ... 11d. ,,

Spouted Bowls
(Basins, White)

diam.
About 12 in. ... 2/3 each.
,, 11 ,, ... 1/7 ,,
,, 10 ,, ... 1/3 ,,
,, 9½ ,, ... 11d. ,,
,, 8½ ,, ... 6½d. ,,
Set of 5, 6/6.

White Jugs

To hold about 1 pint ... 4d. each.
,, ,, 2 ,, ... 5½d. ,,
,, ,, 3½ ,, ... 8d. ,,
Set of 3 jugs, 1/5.

Oval Baking Dishes
(White)

About 7 in. long ... 2/3 doz.
,, 8 ,, ,, ... 3/- ,,
,, 9 ,, ,, ... 3/9 ,,
,, 10 ,, ,, ... 4/- ,,
,, 11 ,, ,, ... 4/9 ,,
,, 12 ,, ,, ... 5/9 ,,
Set of 6, one of each size, 1/11.

Jars
(Brown Hardware)
6d., 8d., 11d. 1/3, and 1/9 each.
Set of 5 Jars, 5/-

**Buff and Gilt Edge Tea
and Breakfast Ware.**

Tea Cups and Saucers ... 2/9 per doz
Breakfast Cups and Saucers 4/9 ,,
Plates ... 2/9 ,,
Tea Plates ... 2/3 ,,
Slop Basin ... 3½d. each.
Sugar ... 3½d. ,,
Large Bread Plate ... 7d. ,,
Milk Jug ... 7d. ,,
Cream Jug ... 4d. ,,
Egg Cups ... 2d. ,,

Jugs
(Toby Philpot in Doulton
Stoneware)

2 quarts ... 2/3 each.
3 pints ... 1/8 ,,
1 quart ... 1/- ,,
1 pint ... 8d. ,,
½ pint ... 5d. ,,

ATKINSON BROTHERS, LITHOGRAPHERS, GRIEL WORKS, HANLEY, ENGLAND.

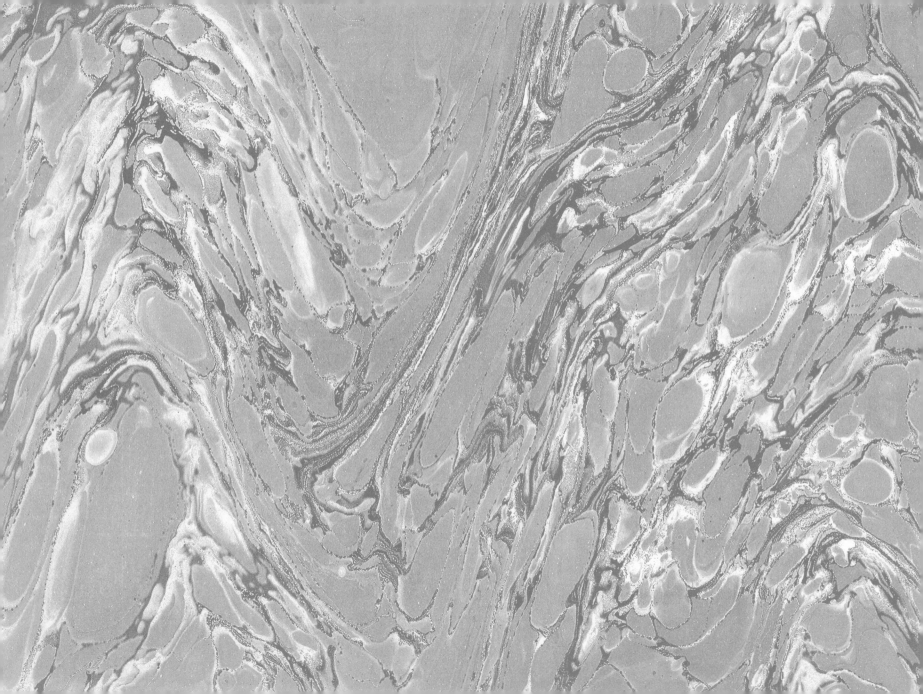